Inter-country adoption

Over the past twenty years, the growing shortage of adoptable infants in Britain and the United States has resulted in a number of couples obtaining their family from abroad, although the effort needed to acquire such a child from another country is enormous. So what exactly are the costs, hazards and emotional difficulties involved, and why do some couples feel that this is their only chance of becoming adoptive parents?

Inter-country Adoption charts the experiences of eight couples who between them have adopted eleven children, ranging in age from four months to seven years, from South America, India and Sri Lanka. The main emphasis of these first-hand accounts is on the events leading up to the decision to adopt from abroad and on the obstacle course which followed and which involved dealing with the authorities in Britain and in the child's country of origin. The final two chapters are by an academic social worker and a parliamentary campaigner, who examine the legal and ethical considerations of inter-country adoption.

This is a lively and highly readable book and will be of great value to social workers, social-policy makers, lawyers and to the general reader with an interest in adoption.

Michael Humphrey has worked closely with the National Association for the Childless and is Reader Emeritus in Psychology at the University of London. **Heather Humphrey** is a research assistant in the Department of Mental Health Sciences at St George's Hospital Medical School.

Inter-country adoption
Practical experiences

Edited by
Michael Humphrey and
Heather Humphrey

Tavistock/Routledge
London and New York

First published 1993
by Routledge
11 New Fetter Lane, London EC4P 4EE

Simultaneously published in the USA and Canada
by Routledge
a division of Routledge, Chapman and Hall, Inc.
29 West 35th Street, New York, NY 10001

Typeset in English Times
by Pat and Anne Murphy, Highcliffe-on-Sea, Dorset
Printed and bound in Great Britain by
Biddles Ltd, Guildford and King's Lynn

British Library Cataloguing in Publication Data
A catalogue record for this book is available from the
British Library.

Library of Congress Cataloging in Publication Data
Inter-country adoption: practical experiences / edited by
   Michael Humphrey and Heather Humphrey.
   p.   cm.
Includes bibliographical references and index.
1. Intercountry adoption.   2. Intercountry adoption –
Great Britain – Case studies.   I. Humphrey, Michael.
II. Humphrey, Heather.
HV875.5.I65   1993
362.7'34–dc20   92-11712
                                                    CIP

ISBN 0–415–08742–2
      0–415–05210–6 (pbk)

Contents

Introduction

This collection of 'travellers' tales' had its origins in a meeting of the executive committee of the National Association for the Childless (NAC) some four years before it finally came to fruition. In Birmingham on a grey Saturday afternoon we were debating what could be done about the dearth of information on inter-country adoption, which was of interest to some of our membership. Though but a fanciful notion for most, we knew that it had been sought or contemplated by some and achieved by a brave few. A detailed fact sheet was proposed as a minimal aim at this stage, but it was thought that a series of first-hand accounts might be more illuminating as a basis for action. Thus the idea for this book was born.

As prospective editors, we were lucky in that some thirty members (mostly married couples) who had adopted from abroad were serving as contacts. We acquired a list of names, addresses and telephone numbers from which we selected those who lived within easy visiting range of our Surrey home. In the event not all could be contacted, and there were some who for various reasons were unable or unwilling to publish their story. We finally had to settle for no more than eight contributors, three of whom were already known to us through the committee. All but one of the remainder were on our list, the exception being a couple who sportingly agreed to take over from friends who were doubtful of their capacity to meet our requirements (mistakenly, we suspect).

The Woodfords were unusual in at least one other respect. All the others had been childless prior to adopting, sometimes for many years. Karina had two nearly adult children from her first marriage but did not want her second marriage to remain childless, especially as her new husband had lost two children in the course of his first marriage. So she was profoundly grateful to her friends for steering them towards Brazil, which had provided a child for two other couples in our small series. She could not at first think of an apt title for her contribution, but her eventual choice of 'The empty nest' is a reminder that the pain of childlessness can take many forms. For some men and women the end of active parenting after twenty or twenty-five years (or possibly longer) may come as an unexpected relief, regardless of the presence or prospect of grandchildren. However, a new partnership may have a wonderfully rejuvenating effect.

Adoption too can bring more than the expected bonus. A subsequent child of the marriage is actually much less common than folklore would suggest, yet it happened quite speedily for two of our couples. And if we discount the single woman and two other women who had undergone a hysterectomy, a 40 per cent incidence of belated fertility is quite remarkable. Call it coincidence if you like, and it would be unethical as well as unrealistic to treat the child adopted from any source as a fertility charm, but those who have virtually given up hope can be in for a pleasant surprise. The prospects are of course brighter for the woman who has found it harder to carry to term than to conceive, as may be inferred from Susie Freeman's lively account of her repeated miscarriages.

The effort needed to aquire a child from abroad is not to be under-estimated. It is also far from cheap, in that it may easily cost at least as much as half the price of a new medium-sized car (to quote from John Hunt, who has compiled guide-lines for the benefit of like-minded couples). This may seem a lot of money, yet as Hunt points out it may be more cost effective than several cycles of *in vitro* fertilization (IVF) and is also more likely to commend itself to bank managers, particularly as compared with a car loan! Much of this expense comes in the form of travel and subsistence, although legal and administrative charges (including the inescapable 'home study') are usually far from negligible. This may help to explain the preponderance of middle-class couples not only in our own experience but almost certainly among inter-country adopters in general. They need to be able to afford the air ticket and much else besides. Moreover, they need also to be able to 'work the system', which calls for more than just material resources.

NAC has a strong middle-class bias, yet only a tiny minority of its members are known to have taken the plunge — the list of thirty contacts, for example, accounted for only about 1 per cent of the membership at the time that it was compiled. Roughly 50 per cent of the total membership could be classified as middle class in terms of the husband's occupation, but it could be that at least 90 per cent of inter-country adopters (as compared with only 30–40 per cent of 'ordinary' adopters) fall into that category. This is why we were keen to include a working-class couple (the Checketts), even if it meant having to compete with the distractions of their rich family life as we elicited their story by word of mouth. Furthermore, what they may have lacked in wealth and education they more than made up for in human qualities.

Interestingly, only the Checketts and Barbara Mostyn found the stamina for a second overseas visit to complete their family, from Sri Lanka and India respectively. The couple who adopted from El Salvador (the Astachnowiczs) acquired their two children simultaneously, although as the youngest contributors in our series they may indeed mean business when they speak now of looking for a third child from abroad. As mentioned above, two couples were subsequently blessed with an unexpected child of their marriage, one of them with the help of IVF. Another two couples (Day and Woodford) had found it hard to reconcile themselves to a one-child family, although the Days were almost past the point of no return once their son had started school. Even in the days when adoption was much easier in Britain, there was always a marked tendency for adopters to content themselves with an only child, often with some misgivings on account of the supposed disadvantages. For those who must now look further afield to adopt it must be tempting to settle for a singleton unless they are lucky enough to pick up a pigeon pair, which is officially frowned upon. There is obviously something to be said for 'geriatric' parenthood in terms of maturity and financial stability; yet a common effect of delayed parenthood – be it voluntary or involuntary – is failure to provide the first child with a sibling. The reasons for this are not hard to find, but it cannot be denied that the adoptee may stand to gain from shared status within the family.

THE FUTURE OF INTER-COUNTRY ADOPTION

There can be no doubt that inter-country adoption has grown in popularity over the past decade. (We may note, for instance, that only one of our informants had adopted before 1980, in this case from Thailand. When ultimately she decided to withdraw from our project it was through expressed concern for the sensitivities of her adolescent daughters.) It can surely be seen as a recent phenomenon in Britain, even if the concept has been familiar for much longer. An informal network of interested parties was established in November 1986 under the banner of STORK; and the Romanian *coup d'état* in December 1989, which turned the spotlight on large numbers of grossly neglected children in local orphanages, has given inter-country adoption a higher profile here and elsewhere. Renewed interest in this route to a much-wanted family is still evident at the time of writing. And whilst Romania is less distant than the other lands to which people have travelled in quest of abandoned orphans, the obstacles have again proved formidable enough to date.

A helpful policy statement from British Agencies for Adoption and Fostering (BAAF) (February 1986) began by acknowledging the absence of reliable statistics. To quote from the opening paragraph, 'Some couples (about 50 a year) apply to the Home Office in the approved manner and seek the necessary entry clearance to bring a child into Britain for this purpose. An increasing number of others, we believe, avoid these procedures altogether simply by acquiring leave to enter for the child on arrival at the airport or simply by carrying the child through unchallenged'. Awareness of this irregularity has led to a demand for greater control over the whole process, notably among social workers and other professionals involved. This is a welcome trend, always provided that it does not create bureaucratic difficulties of a kind that might be expected to dampen the spirit of adventure. We are fortunate in having persuaded Peter Thurnham, MP, at desperately short notice, to provide a statement on the objectives of his parliamentary campaign, launched as our book was nearing completion.

We agree with the BAAF working party and the parliamentary campaigners in their wish to see a specialized agency established for the benefit of couples who at present have to 'go it alone'. This should help to make the obstacle course more manageable, even if it does nothing to reduce the expense. As several of our contributors have made abundantly clear, there are legal formalities to be observed before a child can be removed from its country of origin. This usually entails an extended flight followed by at least a few days' stay; and unless the child is from certain designated countries (mainly Commonwealth or European), the adopting couple will then need to wait for a second court hearing when they return home. It is thus a protracted undertaking and often extremely stressful, but adopting a child even under ideal circumstances is not for the faint-hearted. It is important to bear in mind that adopted children are protected by law, and rightly so. As those responsible for arranging adoptions are inevitably more aware than would-be adopters, in law the interests of the child must take precedence over those of the prospective parents. In other words, adoption has come to be recognized as a service for deprived children rather than for childless couples.

ADOPTIVE PARENTHOOD – A HAZARDOUS ADVENTURE?

This was the title of a paper published by an academic social worker a quarter of a century ago (Kadushin 1966). He argued – not altogether convincingly in our view – that the social characteristics of a typical adoptive family, with its middle-class values and curtailment by a late start, might turn out to be more relevant than any psychological stresses inherent in the adoptive relationship. The question has yet to be finally resolved, although we have done our best to review the evidence impartially in our recent monograph (Humphrey and Humphrey 1988).

It has long been known that pre-adoptive parental deprivation can increase the risk of emotional disturbance and antisocial behaviour in adopted individuals, perhaps especially during adolescence and early adulthood. It therefore makes sense to place children for adoption before they have had time to become attached to temporary care-takers, and more especially without allowing them to languish in an impersonal institution for months if not years on end. Nevertheless adoption can work well enough even when the first few years of a child's life have been devoid of normal parenting, as Tizard (1977) has shown in her study of the effects of early institutional rearing. Yet in general it remains safe to assert that the earlier the adoption the better the outlook, and so it is reassuring to find that only two of the eleven children adopted by our couples were older than six months when they arrived in this country. One of these girls was 8 months old and the other past her second birthday, but both appeared to have settled perfectly well when the families were visited a couple of years later.

In his review of outcome studies of inter-country adoption in the USA and elsewhere, John Triseliotis has drawn attention to some of the difficulties experienced by older children on arrival in their host country, especially when faced with the challenge of adjusting to the demands of school as well as to those of family life. This was to be expected, but there is as yet no clear evidence to suggest that the trans-racial adoption of infants is more hazardous than conventional adoptions. Distressing experiences in the country of origin may well have set the stage for later parenting difficulties in the case of these older children, although usually the adopters know little or nothing about the child's early history.

An extreme example has been provided by Rachel Anderson (1990) in her moving story of Sang, a Vietnamese war orphan of uncertain age but believed to be about 9 years old when he joined her family. In doing so he acquired an older sister, a younger brother and a second brother who could have been older or younger but was in any case too close in age for comfort. She writes:

> From the start the only thing we were absolutely sure of was that we all loved him so much. Despite the fact that he had brought rage, self-destruction, chaos and spiritual despair into our family, we knew we had to hang on to him because he was meant to be with us. But we could never have anticipated the anguish of caring for a child who was profoundly traumatised, irreversibly brain-damaged, and whose small, malnourished body frequently disintegrated into uncontrollable violence.
>
> (Anderson 1990)

That the Andersons' marriage survived was a minor miracle, and called at one stage for periods of marital separation with mothering and fathering as alternating regimes.

It would seem that despite his continuing learning difficulties, the intrinsically lovable Sang was finally absorbed into his adoptive family without causing lasting damage to other members, but for a long time it was touch and go. Such uplifting accounts of triumph over major adversity deserve to be published but must not be allowed to deter less intrepid spirits. The Andersons were not after all seeking relief from their childlessness. Not all damaged children can be expected to learn how to cope with the intimacies of family life, and doubts had been expressed about Sang's adoptability even before the matter was put to the test. But for the courage and persistence of this particular family, he would undoubtedly have remained in long-term care.

Those who argue against the propriety of inter-country adoption are sometimes obsessed with the need to preserve a child's cultural heritage. But what if the only obvious alternative to adoption into a more affluent society is a short and disastrous life? There have to be adequate safeguards against kidnapping; and where the child has not been orphaned or abandoned the mother's consent (or parents' consent in the case of a married couple) must be verified. In an ideal world no parent would ever be put under any pressure to release a child for adoption, yet the realities of the Third World can be harsh. If the child could choose in full awareness of the available options, what kind of choice would make most sense? Is it better to risk a life of misery in the child's home country, which may include chronic malnutrition, disease and premature death, or should the opportunity for healthy growth and self-fulfilment be seized, albeit in an alien culture? For inter-country adoption to work best, the decision has to be taken by others on the child's behalf. And one has only to read Barbara Mostyn's comments on 7-year-old Joshua's 'human potential' (fine singing voice, lovely sense of colour, texture and design, avid interest in wildlife) to be persuaded that his rescue from oblivion will have gained him far more than he lost.

IDENTITY AND RACIAL AWARENESS

On the whole, social workers have been less than enthusiastic about inter-country adoption in recent years. A commonly expressed objection is that the children involved will grow up with an inadequate or incomplete sense of their own identity. They will come up against racial prejudice in the local community, and in extreme cases may even be driven to feel like social outcasts. They may see themselves as close enough to their adoptive parents in many other ways, yet at the same time experience feelings of alienation, of not belonging. What can be done to protect them?

Both Barbara Mostyn and the Astachnowiczs record having chosen to live in a multicultural area, in the hope that this would serve as a partial safeguard for their children as they grew up. Admittedly only four of the eleven children in our study had reached school age at the time of our visit, and then only just. If there is such a thing as an adolescent identity crisis – and this has not been universally acknowledged – it lay well ahead for all these children. But these were well-educated parents (about half were graduates) who already had some idea of how to play their cards when the time came. Most if not all of them were explicitly aware that in adopting a child from abroad they were in effect adopting both the child and its cultural heritage for life. It therefore paid to choose the country with this point in mind, since in time to come it would be a central focus for planning visits to libraries or exhibitions and cinemas or theatres, meeting new people, and returning to the country of origin for excursions. The family's relationship with the country would need to be one of affection and respect rather than antipathy and distrust.

As it happens, we still know all too little about the detailed processes of identity formation in children and young people, be they black, brown or white, and whatever their mode of upbringing. Elsewhere (Humphrey and Humphrey 1986, 1989) we have argued that ignorance of one's origins is fully compatible with healthy self-esteem where the child has grown up in a sympathetic and loving adoptive home. It is primarily those with an unsatisfactory experience of adoption who are likely to develop an obsessive curiosity about their ancestry, leading to a compulsion to search for their biological relatives. These are the adoptees who hit the headlines and thereby create bad publicity for what is otherwise a socially acceptable form of substitute care. Children adopted from abroad are of course at a particularly grave disadvantage when it comes to filling the lacunae of their murky past. Their adoptive parents cannot pretend to have brought them into the world, but equally they are seldom in a position to provide reassuring background information. When all has gone well they will have left their children in no doubt of their lovability and intrinsic worth, which is a mark of being valued for who they are, and not for how they happen to have come into the family.

In theory, all adopted individuals are confronted sooner or later with the dilemma of their dual parentage. Their sense of self may be heavily influenced by feedback from 'significant others'; yet it is quite normal for them to wonder about their genetic make-up, especially during crucial phases of development or periods of external stress. Adoptive status calls for some understanding of why some children are 'released' or 'surrendered' by their original parent(s) (not 'given up' or 'abandoned', unless this is an essential part of the story). Only through skilled communication on the part of the adopters will they learn to appreciate their place in the world and feel comfortable about their roots in another culture. Adults whose personal resources allow them to pursue inter-country adoption may well have the edge over others who are less strongly motivated. The sheer delight of our own informants in having found their children at such daunting emotional cost is a memorable feature of their stories. As an illustration of what it takes to battle against seemingly intractable odds the story of Audrey and David Wilson is hard to beat.

THE CURRENT SCENARIO

Despite growing concern over the need for strict regulation which has been reinforced by the recent parliamentary campaign, there is something to be said for a more flexible approach. Over the past twelve months there have been press reports of, for example, German or Swedish couples collecting children from Romania without fuss or bother, whilst British couples were delayed or even discouraged by tiresome protocol. The need for prior entry clearance is a case in point. Law-abiding citizens who believe in acting on official advice may find themselves waiting for months as their documents are shuffled between government departments, long after bold opportunists have managed to bluff their way through the immigration authorities. There seems to have been no recorded instance of an infant without a visa being denied entry as long as the couple's passports are in order; and increasing familiarity with this loophole in the system has made it more and more tempting to take short cuts.

The obligatory 'home study' was always potentially a source of difficulty but has recently become a much more serious obstacle. This has to be carried out by a local authority-based social worker, whose task it is to enquire into the couple's personal history and present circumstances with a view to reporting on their suitability as adoptive parents. The investigation will include health and police checks as well as character references. A home study report is required by most reputable adoption agencies abroad before they will allocate a named child, but without a named child the local authority is not obliged to carry out the study.

Until recently, a way round this impasse was for prospective adopters to commission a report from an independent social worker as a basis for negotiation with overseas authorities, which if successful would enable them to apply to their local authority for an official home study. Sadly, however, this loophole was closed by a Department of Health directive (28 September 1990) requiring local authorities to conduct their own home studies *ab initio* and supported by one from the Foreign Office asking overseas authorities to disregard private home studies. It is still too early to assess the full impact of this restriction, which was presumably part of the impetus for the parliamentary campaign.

Our own informants did not face this difficulty because the most recent of these adoptions was early in 1990, when there was still scope for private enterprise. A careful reading of the stories to follow will reveal that attitudes to protocol varied from couple to couple, as might be expected of even a small and relatively homogeneous group. Some were anxious to observe the correct procedure come what may, others were willing to cut corners (and, who knows, may even have taken a mischievous delight in so doing). Yet we would question whether the latest ruling is wholly acceptable even if the pre-existing situation left too much room for manœuvre.

It could also be argued that the assessment process itself has become unduly rigorous. Couples attending infertility clinics are not expected to convince doctors of their fitness for parenthood, desirable as this might be in some cases especially where donor gametes are involved. Because the interests of the adoptee are paramount, the adopting couple must be ready to submit to a relentless and not always courteous inquisition. One London borough known to us likes to subject would-be adopters to ten hours of group discussion followed by another ten hours of individual scrutiny, at the end of which their names *may* be added to a waiting list but with no guaranteed outcome. Couples are handled tactfully so far as we know, but is it surprising that some turn to foreign countries in the hope of expediting their quest for a child? However, this will not absolve them from a detailed appraisal of their domestic circumstances, as we have seen.

The skills of social workers have become more finely tuned as the level of their training has hopefully improved over the past few decades. This era has also witnessed a change of emphasis on the qualities required of adoptive parents. Less weight is now given to piety and social convention, more to warmth of personality and mutual devotion. In the realm of family life as elsewhere, prediction can never be an exact science, and some adoptions can fail to live up to their early promise just as others can flourish against all the odds (there must be other examples apart from the legendary Sang). Those responsible for vetting adoptive applicants have no easy task, and it could be that social workers have attracted more than their fair share of criticism.

Whilst writing this introduction our attention was drawn to a press report of an adverse experience of vetting for inter-country adoption (*Daily Telegraph*, 22 February 1991). 'If you want to be allowed to adopt', wrote the injured party, 'you have to agree with whatever is said to you by the social worker, and be subjected to intrusive and bathetic Cosmopolitan-questionnaire psychology'. She did not elaborate on the content of the questionnaire, but the journalist had been reliably informed by a personal friend that one of the key questions asked was 'Do you wear knickers?' We did not think to enquire how many of our own adoptive mothers were thus equipped for their chosen way of life, and we would like in any case to believe that the story is apocryphal. But sadly it does nothing to enhance the credibility of a much maligned profession. If social workers are to play a significant role in regulating inter-country adoption they will need to find some way of improving their image!

In conclusion, it is our modest hope that these first-hand accounts will convey an authentic flavour of what it means to adopt a child from abroad. Prior to the Romanian purge the majority of successful bids had been made to the following ten countries: Brazil, Bolivia, Chile, Columbia, Ecuador, El Salvador, India, Peru, Sri Lanka and Thailand (STORK/NAC fact sheet on inter-country adoption, August 1989). Half of these countries are represented in what follows, namely Brazil (three cases), Columbia, El Salvador, India and Sri Lanka (two cases). This fact sheet (like the notes on individual countries) was designed as a 'general guide to the most relevant issues and necessary steps concerning inter-country adoption'. It could not hope to be definitive because the situation in the various countries is in a constant state of flux. The same limitation applies to our book, which cannot serve as a blueprint for readers wishing to explore the same routes. But it may at least help to demonstrate what *could* be done between 1983 and 1990, given the refusal to be beaten. And the process appeared to work most smoothly when a couple were hot on the trail of others' footsteps, like the Woodfords who were exceptionally well briefed.

A final word about our contributors. None are professional writers, even if one or two have written to a professional standard in the course of their work. Within broad guidelines they were given a free hand, and as editors we have intervened as little as possible. Consequently there is no semblance of uniformity about these travellers' tales even if recurring themes emerge, as we hope they do. Some are humorous and light-hearted, others solemn and circumstantial. What helps to unite them (we think) is a common thread of human enterprise, and indeed perhaps courage would not be too strong a word.

Michael and Heather Humphrey
March 1991

REFERENCES

Anderson, R. (1990) *For the Love of Sang*, Oxford: Lion.

Humphrey, H. and Humphrey, M. (1989) 'Damaged identity and the search for kinship in adult adoptees', *British Journal of Medical Psychology* 62: 301–9.

Humphrey, M. and Humphrey, H. (1986) 'A fresh look at genealogical bewilderment', *British Journal of Medical Psychology* 59: 133–40.

—— (1988) *Families with a Difference: Varieties of Surrogate Parenthood*, London: Routledge & Kegan Paul.

Kadushin, A. (1966) 'Adoptive parenthood: a hazardous adventure?', *Social Work* 11: 30–9.

Tizard, B. (1977) *Adoption: A Second Chance*, London: Open Books.

1 From San Salvador to Hackney

Claire and Andrew Astachnowicz

*Claire and Andrew Astachnowicz are both 29 years old and live in
North London. They met in 1978 and married in 1984. Andrew is a
lawyer and Claire used to work as the editor of a Norwegian trade
magazine as well as doing freelance legal editing. In January 1988 they
adopted Veronica (2¼ years) and Benedict (3 months) from El
Salvador.*

At the beginning of 1987 we had been trying unsuccessfully for two
years to start a family. We decided to consult our GP who recommended that we be referred to an infertility clinic. We got several
books on infertility from the library which gave accounts of causes,
treatments and descriptions by various couples of their experience of
infertility and details of success rates.

We both felt very uneasy about resorting to medical solutions to
form our family. As Catholics, we were aware of the Church's views
on some of the treatments available and this did nothing to endear us
to this option. Above all we increasingly felt that in a world with
between one and two hundred million street children we could not
really justify the huge expense, ours or the State's, of perhaps
scientifically producing our 'own' child. There seems to be something
questionable about a society where the needs of so many children in
the Third World go unheeded and the childless go to such enormous
lengths to produce their own biological children. We would never
condemn anyone for doing this, but equally we believed we could not
really justify it in our own minds.

We had in the past talked of adoption as a means of adding to our
family and so we did not really find it hard to make this transition. We
did not feel that adoption could only be thought of as a last resort
measure when all else failed. In addition I had always regarded
pregnancy as a means to an end and, despite current views, did not

really feel it would be a particularly uplifting experience. Adoption became an increasingly obvious answer.

I will say that we realized from the outset that mere altruism towards abandoned or orphaned children was not enough. We had to be sure that we could truly love a child that was not our 'own'. A view of the global family and a revulsion against poverty would not in themselves be good enough reasons to form an adopted family. However, we wanted to be parents and did not have strong feelings or needs to produce biological children. We believed we would be good parents, as we had a stable and very happy relationship and financial security – we felt we had much to offer a child. In addition we wanted the experience of nurturing and caring for children – a life without children was for us quite unthinkable.

Initially we made enquiries in the UK. We knew that at 27 years old we had not passed any age limits and felt we would be suitable candidates for adoption. We went to see the adoption unit of our local social services and were immediately informed by a social worker that we would only be considered for white children as there was a total ban on trans-racial adoption in our area. We looked through a book called *Be My Parent*, but most of the children were black or of mixed race. The social worker informed us that we could not even be considered for one Anglo-Asian toddler included in the book, as such a child would be considered 'black'. We left the offices and walked home, and the world suddenly seemed a very mad place. I thought of our large empty house and all that we had to offer as parents and felt incredibly depressed. I then wrote to a voluntary agency who, after six weeks, replied inviting us to a video showing in six months' time. This did not seem a very inspiring response either.

Around this time we began to think increasingly about overseas adoption. Some time previously I had bought a magazine which included an article on overseas adoption. I contacted the National Association for the Childless who sent me their information pack on inter-country adoption (ICA). I rang a contact name in Leeds and spoke to a lady who had adopted two children from abroad.

It was an extremely moving experience, and my eyes filled with tears as she described her enormous love for these two children. She said she had had years of painful and hopeless infertility treatment, but now felt very glad that she had never had her 'own' child because then she would not have adopted her children, who she believed were the ones she was really meant to have.

We continued to make enquiries about ICA and to learn as much as we could on the subject. We also began to mention our plans to some close friends and relatives. Most of them, including both our families, were very supportive. However, some told us in no uncertain terms that they felt ICA was quite wrong. From what we had read we realized from very early on that it is a very contentious issue and so we were not particularly surprised.

By this stage we had contacted the El Salvador Embassy in London who had recommended a particular lawyer working with the Salvadorean Child Welfare Department. They assured us that she was bona fide and they had no hesitation in giving us her name. They also informed us that El Salvador had many abandoned and orphaned children, due to the various economic problems there and the terrible earthquake it suffered in 1986. We wrote to her, and within three weeks she had replied saying she would help us in adopting a child. We were surprised by the speed at which this had been accomplished and wanted to take some time to consider our next step.

One of the arguments we encountered was that in removing a child from its country of origin we were robbing that child of its 'cultural identity'. Our reading about El Salvador and its many problems made this a quite ludicrous argument. The country was in its seventh year of a very bloody and unresolved civil war which had displaced around a quarter of the population. Many had fled to neighbouring countries where they lived in squalid refugee camps. Many others had gone to the capital where they set up home in the overcrowded shanty towns. There is no welfare benefit and with 60 per cent unemployment many had to resort to begging in order to survive. We learned from information packs sent to us from various charities that 20 per cent of children die before their fifth birthday, 75 per cent of children suffer from malnutrition and only 10 per cent receive more than a few years' basic education. So to talk of robbing such children of their cultural heritage seemed to us indulgent western 'armchair' idealism of the worst kind.

The problems of El Salvador, we learned, are deeply rooted in its history. They are more than the economic problems of an undeveloped country. Our critics felt that western aid was the solution, meaning that if we had a genuine concern for the orphaned children of El Salvador we should have donated the money we later spent in legal fees to relevant charities. In fact hardly any UK agencies have projects in El Salvador, as human rights and charity workers have been in the front line facing persecution by extreme groups in the country.

We also had to address the issue of whether it was proper for us as white 'parents' to raise brown Hispanic children. We both felt it was essential to bring children up with a strong sense of their racial origin and self-worth, but we did not feel we had to be the same colour as them in order to do this.

Both Andy's parents are Polish and he is the first generation born in this country. He was brought up in a totally Polish environment and spoke no English until he went to school, where he was sometimes told to 'go back to his own country' and so on. We therefore felt that he was uniquely placed to relate to our adopted children and to support them when they inevitably faced similar encounters.

Andy says that the only time he ever felt any identity crisis was when Poland played England in the World Cup at Wembley. He still refuses to admit to me which team he actually supported, as he says he could never be on the losing side! In many ways a dual cultural background does mean that a child can experience the best of both.

We live and plan to stay in an inner city London borough which has a huge ethnic population. Our children would meet children from many different races and would thus not look racially different from many of their classmates. We also felt that it would enhance our family life to have a Salvadorean element in our household. It would give us and our children an exciting extra dimension to explore together.

The arguments against trans-racial adoption seemed to us flimsy and not based on much real evidence, apart from the results of a few ill-advised placements in the 1960s. We realized that ICA children would grow up with a different value system to the one they would have had if they had stayed in their country of origin, but we could not believe such children would spend their lives in a state of permanent identity crisis because of this.

A few friends warned us against baby-buying/child-stealing, and dealing with corrupt profiteers. Even our most basic investigations into ICA showed us that overseas adoption, like everything else in this world, can be done in a right way and a wrong way. Various basic guidelines became apparent, e.g. always deal with reputable agencies/lawyers who obtain an adoption/guardianship/custody order that includes proof of relinquishment by the natural mother or a proper court statement of abandonment. We were advised to be wary of lawyers who charged huge fees — five-figure numbers are clearly much more than reasonable legal recompense. We were told to deal with agencies/lawyers who insisted on a full 'home study' being done on us by a fully-qualified social worker.

This advice was repeated again and again in all the information we read on ICA as well as by couples who had already adopted from abroad with whom we had lengthy telephone conversations. Only the most hapless couple could complete an overseas adoption and claim to be unaware of these guidelines.

Having examined these arguments in great depth we did not find any of them in the least compelling. We did, however, seriously consider them as part of our evaluation of ICA as a solution to our childlessness.

We now felt that this was the course we wanted to embark upon, and set about arranging for the long list of documents which our Salvadorean lawyer had sent to be compiled. She required a home study, a psychological report, references from our bank, employers, three friends and a priest, a medical report from our doctor for us both, and police clearance as well as our birth and marriage certificates. When I rang a social worker who had been recommended to me by other ICA couples, she said she could not promise to take us on until we had gathered together and sent all the other documents to her, which seemed fair enough. I spent a few weeks in a whirl of visiting doctors, priests, friends, etc. We arranged to see a psychologist recommended to us by other couples who had adopted from El Salvador, as he was aware of the various requirements the El Salvador government stipulated in psychological reports on adopting couples, which included a set of 566 questions to be answered 'true' or 'false' (the Minnesota Multiphasic Personality Inventory). We also visited him for a lengthy interview in which he asked us detailed questions about our attitudes towards adoption, our own relationship and material resources, etc. About a week after our visit he sent us a very favourable report.

Having compiled all the documents, I contacted the social worker again. We arranged a day when she would come on a visit of inspection. I sent her copies of all the documents that we had gathered as well as an essay from each of us about our lives to date. This was fascinating to do, and I think we learned a lot about each other from what we had written. The social worker came to see us and spent most of the day in our house. Initially she looked around the house and went into every room and the garden to check that we had a suitable family home. The rest of her visit was spent in discussions with the two of us and all the ramifications of adopting from abroad. We also visited her several times and the discussion continued along similar lines. We soon received her report, which again recommended us highly and said we would be good adoptive parents.

Although this period of compiling documents seemed hard work it was easy compared to what lay ahead. We were so busy that we did not have much time for worrying. We continued to read all we could lay our hands on about El Salvador – archaeology books, travel accounts, history books and contemporary political studies. We joked to each other that at least if we did not end up adopting we would apply to go on Mastermind with El Salvador as our special subject!

We then took all the documents to a Notary Public for legal notarization. The Notary Public also arranged for our documents to be legalized at the Foreign Office and then authenticated by the El Salvador Embassy. We then went to the USA for a three-week holiday.

At the start, the process seemed like a huge mountain that we had to climb and we now felt we had begun to take a few steps upward. It was compulsive once we started – for ten months I thought of little else. In many ways I see that as a strength, because in order to achieve ICA you have to be totally dedicated.

We returned from our holiday and I was worried that we would find a letter saying it was all off. So I left Andy struggling on the pavement with all the luggage and flew into the house and tore through all our post looking for letters with a Salvadorean stamp. There was indeed one, and it was in Spanish. We had a furious row and I insisted that Andy rang the Embassy to get them to translate it. He did, and it turned out to be merely a request to send off our documents soon.

We sent off all our stamped documents – plus a Power of Attorney drawn up by the Embassy giving our lawyer authority to act on our behalf in the El Salvador courts – to El Salvador by a courier service, which managed to lose the lot. So we had a harrowing few days shouting at the couriers to find them. They were eventually traced to Salvador, Brazil. They were retrieved and delivered to our lawyer, after which I made a point of writing to 'El Salvador, Central America'.

The next few days were very strange, as we did not know if a child/children would be placed in days, weeks or months. We had specified that if possible we wanted to adopt a baby and a young child. Three weeks later the phone rang – it was a bad line and a voice with a strong Spanish accent explained that he was ringing on behalf of our lawyer as he acted as her translator. He said, 'We have a girl of two and a baby boy of five days – do you want to be considered for them?' My heart pounded and I asked if I could call back in a few minutes. Andy and I said yes, yes, to each other and scribbled a list of questions. Andy rang back and spoke to Felipe, the translator, again. We were told that both the mothers were single and had other children to support. Being very poor they were in the sad position of having to relinquish one child to keep destitution at bay. Our adoption of these two children would be heard in the Salvadorean Minors Court and we were told to ring back in two months' time when we would hopefully be given a date to collect them. The lawyer estimated that the hearing would be within the two months and anticipated, having read all our translated documents, that an adoption order would be made in our favour. We both realized that, prior to the adoption orders being granted, either mother would be able to change her mind and keep the child.

We spent the rest of the evening in a furore of excitement and happiness. We tried to picture the children, and I rang some family and close friends who were all delighted and eager to hear all the details.

I was given the name of another couple who were shortly to go out to El Salvador to collect their child. I telephoned them and they promised to take some photographs of the children if possible. Several weeks later on their return, they rang us to say they had seen the little girl, who was called Veronica, and they had taken some photos of her. She was living with the lawyer and was apparently a lovely and friendly little girl. They had not been able to see the baby boy as he was with a foster mother in another part of the city. Anyway, a few days later the photos of Veronica arrived and she looked beautiful, with huge brown eyes and lovely glossy hair. No photograph has ever been looked at more. I kept it in my bag and would gaze at it on buses, trains and tubes.

This was the real wait. We knew that in El Salvador many miles away were the two children we longed to see and be with. I thought of them every hour, every minute. I wondered how they were, what time it was in El Salvador, what they looked like, and so on.

As time passed I began to get very fatalistic in case it all went wrong. The situation seemed so vulnerable – hoping for so much to go right for us in a little unhappy country thousands of miles away. Andy was incredibly supportive and calm. He just kept assuring me that everything would be all right. I know now that he was as worried as I was inside but decided it would be better for me if he concealed his fears.

The longest two months of our lives came to an end at last and we telephoned our lawyer. Someone who answered said she had moved house. We were very worried by this and contacted her translator. He told us what had happened. The lawyer's house had been broken into by armed men who had held her hostage for several hours. The family were so frightened that they had moved to another house along with our little Veronica, who was living with them.

Several days later I rang again. Our lawyer was with the translator, who told me that ten days before an adoption order had been made in our favour for us to be the parents of both children. So they were now our legal children under Salvadorean law. He told me that Veronica kept saying 'her mummy was coming in a big aeroplane to take her up to the clouds!'

The lawyer wanted another Power of Attorney from us to enable her to get the children's passports from the Salvadorean Immigration Office. The Power of Attorney and a letter were already on their way to us. On receipt we had to take it to the El Salvador Embassy to get them to draw it up in its current legal form. We did not receive it for several weeks and then discovered the Embassy was closed for the Christmas break until early January. This meant more frustrating delay, and we spent a rotten Christmas thinking of the two children we had legally adopted 10,000 miles away.

Along with the Power of Attorney form that arrived just before Christmas was a detailed letter giving us information about our children and their background. Veronica, the letter told us, was the daughter of a 20-year-old student called Elsa. Her boyfriend had left her to go to the USA when she was six months pregnant. She had left her parents and nine younger siblings to come to the capital to study during the day and to work in the evenings in order to support herself. Immediately after the birth Veronica was handed over to her grand-parents who were to care for her, as it was impractical for Elsa to do so. So Elsa remained in San Salvador while Veronica was cared for by her extended family in Chalchupa, an impoverished area in the north of the country. Elsa sent home most of her earnings to support her little daughter. Unfortunately she had another liaison which resulted in the birth of a son in January 1987. Her parents were very angry and said they wanted nothing more to do with her and accordingly returned Veronica to her care. Elsa's situation was now very serious. She had two small children to care for alone, as neither father offered any support whatsoever. Her small son was being cared for by his paternal aunt. At first she took Veronica along with her to work, but she was threatened with dismissal for doing this. So Elsa took the sad decision to put Veronica up for adoption. It must have been particu-larly wrenching to part with a child she had supported and looked after for two years. She took Veronica along to the Salvadorean Child Welfare Department who referred her on to our lawyer. Veronica had been living with the lawyer for five months.

Benedict, as we had decided to call him, was the son of an 18-year-old girl. From her earnings as a baker she had to support various members of her extended family. She already had a 2-year-old son by another father. Benedict was the result of a casual relationship, and the girl had come to the despairing conclusion that she would be unable to support him as well as all her other dependants.

Both mothers had been informed that the children were to be adopted by us and were to live in England. Their decision to give their children up for adoption must have been heart-breaking, and we can never underestimate their sacrifice. At the same time we are both convinced that they made a brave and courageous choice, as in the circumstances it was better to put the children up for adoption than to keep them and watch them go steadily downhill.

Anyway, to return to our situation. The Embassy reopened at last and on 7 January 1988 we went there and signed the Power of Attorney. We sent it off at once to our lawyer in El Salvador. Three days later we rang her and were told to come on 24 January. At last, after nearly three months of waiting, we had a date and some certainty that we would see our children soon. We immediately set to work arranging air flights and we booked to go via Miami. The next two weeks were spent packing and making all the other arrangements.

Finally on 23 January we left Gatwick for Miami feeling very glad to be on our way at last. The next time we would stand on English soil our two children would be with us. We arrived in Miami in the evening and went straight to our hotel. After a restless night we woke up – on the day our lives would change utterly. We dressed – the last time we would be able to do so leisurely for many years! We went to the airport and checked in for our flight to San Salvador. We spent the next few hours wandering around the airport feeling very weird. I can never properly explain how we felt except to say everything you can imagine – excited, happy, terrified, nervous, full of anticipation. It was a totally unique human experience.

On board the plane were many members of the Salvadorean upper classes, who all looked very affluent and beautiful. There were a few Americans aboard who seemed to be either nuns or rather thuggish-looking men. I was feeling extremely sick by now and could not eat a morsel, so Andy, who was feeling much calmer, ate both our lunches! We flew over the Florida Keys and Cuba and before long we reached the coastline of Honduras and saw the first of many volcanoes. We stopped briefly at Tegucigalpa, the capital of Honduras.

After take-off we were in the final stages of the flight and landed at Ilopango Airport at 4 p.m. It was a lovely sunny day when we disembarked. One of the first things we saw was a huge government propaganda poster showing terrible photographs of people who had lost limbs from stepping on guerilla landmines. The caption read,

'Here are the innocent victims of El Salvador', and it was a ghoulish reminder of the war. We went through Immigration, which was full of soldiers carrying machine guns, and into the airport lounge, our hearts thumping in anticipation. Immediately the lawyer's husband and the translator greeted us and took us to their car. The trip to San Salvador was amazing and took around forty minutes. The road was a stretch of the Pan American highway and almost empty. I was glad I had not eaten any lunch, as I was feeling very nervous by now and was sure I would have been violently sick. As we approached San Salvador we saw the first shanty towns and then between the volcanoes the city itself. There were buses full of people and little houses seemed to be crammed everywhere. Some of them were just made from pieces of wood with a few plastic sacks thrown over the tops as roofs. Many buildings still showed signs of extensive earthquake damage.

We were now both feeling extremely excited, knowing we would see our children within the hour. We got to the hotel and checked in, and waited anxiously in our room with Felipe and Sebastian, the lawyer's husband. How many times I had imagined this first meeting with our children, and we were now so close to it. I was in mid-sentence when the door opened and Veronica and Benedict were brought in. I felt a sob pass through me as I saw Veronica – she looked much more fragile than I had imagined. The lawyer brought her over to me and said I was to be her mummy. Veronica was so composed and I was struck at once by her amazing dignity. I took her on my lap and she said 'Coca Cola'. Benedict was handed to Andy and my first impression of him was how thin he was. He looked like a tiny Chinese old-age pensioner. His face was particularly thin and he looked all ears and nose. He was dressed in a heavy woollen outfit and looked very red and hot. His breathing was wheezy and he seemed in some discomfort.

So there we all were, crammed into this small hotel room: the four of us, the lawyer, Marta, Sebastian, Felipe, Marta's sister and a maid who Veronica had nicknamed 'Chia'. I held Benedict – he was so small and sweet with lovely brown eyes and I longed for everyone to go so we could dress him in something cooler and feed him. Veronica seemed very much at home and pranced around entertaining us and demanding Coca Cola endlessly.

Marta, Felipe and Andy went through a huge pile of papers – our Salvadorean adoption documents. She explained them all to Andy. I was in too much of a daze to take it all in. I sat looking at our daughter and baby son, unable to believe that they were both finally with us.

Eventually everyone left, and we both set to work boiling kettles, making up bottles. We dressed Benedict in a cooler outfit. Marta had given us various medicines for his chest as he had a 'cold'. He looked even more thin when we took his clothes off and his nails were long and dirty. There was more dirt behind his ears. Veronica played contentedly with her toys and tried to communicate with us. Andy entertained her by pulling funny faces and so within an hour she had christened him 'loco papi' – 'loony daddy' which she thought was hilarious. She was very taken with her little brother, who she called 'Sito'. He is still known to us by this nickname.

Dark came early and we all collapsed into bed. We woke to find the sun streaming through our windows. We got both children dressed, Benedict was fed and we dressed ourselves – it took us nearly three hours to get ready to go into the hotel restaurant for breakfast. What a contrast to twenty-four hours earlier!

Later that day Andy took Veronica to the supermarket and I sat alone with Benedict. He lay in my lap and we both gazed intensely at one another. He smiled and cooed at me endlessly, and at the risk of sounding corny I felt he was saying to me, 'I am so glad you have turned up to look after me'. Later we all went into the hotel garden and took lots of photographs to remember our first full day together.

The next day we were taken by our hosts to the US Embassy to obtain transit visas for both children, as we would again be spending one night in Miami on the way back. The US Embassy was a huge concrete bunker and was covered in wire mesh to keep bombs out. It was surrounded by Salvadorean armed soldiers. There was an enormous queue of Salvadoreans who were hoping to get US visas to enable them to leave the country. We were told that this queue starts to form at 3 a.m. every morning. As we were British we were allowed in straight away, and although we both felt uneasy about this we realized that waiting for hours in the hot sun with a tiny baby and toddler would be grim. We went into a courtyard full of soldiers holding machine guns and were all frisked, even little Benedict. Our bags were also searched. The atmosphere was very tense and I was trembling – I realized I am no hero when it comes down to it! After a fifteen-minute wait we were ushered into a small bullet-proof cubicle where a US embassy official looked at our passports and said, 'So you are subjects of her Majesty's Britannic Isles'. We explained we wanted transit visas for our adopted children and handed over all our adoption documents. The embassy official said he would have to check their legality with the courts concerned and added that if there was any doubt about their authenticity we would not be allowed into the USA with our two small Salvadorean citizens. We left the Embassy and Marta returned later to collect our documents and the children's passports, which now included a three-month US transit visa.

The next day Marta, Sebastian and Felipe returned to take us out for a meal. A maid came along to act as babysitter. However, Veronica was having none of this and insisted on coming along with us. We had an enjoyable evening chatting about the children and their backgrounds. We had wanted to meet both their mothers but the atmosphere in San Salvador was strained, and we were told it would not be a good idea as movements to outlying areas would be dangerous for foreigners. We were both very sorry about this and I still wish we could have met the two women to whom we owe so much.

The next day we were to start our journey home, and Marta told us she would not be able to see us again as she had to spend the day in court. So we said our goodbyes to this woman to whom we are forever indebted. She took Veronica in her arms and said goodbye to her with tears in her eyes. She had looked after her devotedly for five months and told us that she was like a daughter to her. Marta believed in Veronica and recognized, as we had done in four days, what a bright, well-adjusted and amazingly lovable child she is. I said that one day she would see Veronica again and Marta nodded her appreciation.

So our meal ended and we were driven back to the hotel. It was still only 7 p.m., but dusk was already falling. Along the pavements soldiers hovered and occasionally pulled over vehicles to check the identity cards of the occupants. The city seemed even more creepy and weird and I was glad we would all be leaving soon. However, part of me also felt very sad that we could not have seen more of the country, but El Salvador was so unsafe as to make that out of the question. It is supposed to be a lovely country with a beautiful coastline. I hoped that one day it would be safe and the four of us would come back for a long holiday and really explore the country.

The next day Felipe and Sebastian came to collect us to drive us to the airport. As usual the street children danced around the cars and every time we stopped some of them would rush up and silently put their outstretched hands through the windows. They never spoke, but stood gazing intensely at us. Their faces were wizened and dirty and their beautiful black hair matted and unkempt. Whenever I think of them I am filled with total horror that anyone, let alone those lovely children, should have to live like that.

It was strange knowing that our two children were so close to leaving the country of their birth, and stranger still that they were so blissfully unaware of the fact. Veronica, as usual, took it all in her stride and pointed excitedly to everything that caught her eye. We reached the airport and checked in and were soon on board waiting for take-off. The children fell asleep, so during this poignant moment of leaving El Salvador they both lay sleeping in our arms. We circled over the fields and mountains and I wondered if the four of us would ever be able to return to that beautiful and unhappy land. We had gone there as a couple and were now leaving as a family with the two children that defied all our wildest dreams and hopes.

Veronica woke up and was very excited by the aeroplane. As we approached Miami she sat on Andy's lap gazing out of the window at the lights below and saying 'avion' over and over again with great delight. Benedict sat smiling on my lap with his beloved dummy in his mouth. At Miami, US Immigration, suspicious of a plane full of Salvadoreans, seemed particularly officious. However, we soon got through and went straight to our hotel. Veronica wasted no time in discovering the bathroom taps which she thought were very thrilling and would not let us turn them off, so our bathroom was soon flooded! Andy rang my father and stepmother to confirm that we had got to Miami, and then we all went to bed.

The next day we went to the airport in the early afternoon to wait for our evening flight back to the UK, and found a nursery where we installed ourselves. Veronica was her usual good-natured self and we took it in turns to show her the aeroplanes which she loved. She had been wonderful from the first moment we met her. She showed no fear or resentment of us at all and behaved with total self-composure, treating the whole experience in the most amazingly positive way. It was as if she trusted in us completely right from the start, and that was very humbling for us both. She was cheerful, funny, lovable, sweet to Benedict and eager to learn. She was, with our coaxing, already saying a few English words. She has my admiration and respect forever – she is a total survivor. Benedict, despite his tiny body, was a gorgeous and happy baby, always smiling and cooing at us. He drank his bottle constantly to make up for his incomplete diet prior to our arrival.

That evening our flight back to England took off – we were tired of travelling by now and longed to be home. It was a never-ending nine hours and I felt sick with worry about our forthcoming encounter with British Immigration. Andy was very calm and kept telling me it would be all right, but I got increasingly dramatic and said that if necessary we would all return to El Salvador to live if Immigration refused to let our children in.

At Gatwick we made our way straight to the UK Non-Passports channel and handed all our adoption papers to the man at the desk. He understood Spanish and studied them all. He asked us why we had not got Home Office permission, and Andy said that the situation in El Salvador was worsening and we wanted to get the children out. The immigration official replied that that was 'fair enough' and added that he would give us a three-month entry visa for both children. So with a huge sense of relief we went into the arrivals lounge, where my father and stepmother were waiting. I fell into my father's arms and burst into tears. Veronica was in the meantime making herself known to my stepmother and chattering away gaily. They drove us back to London and helped us carry our now sleeping children upstairs to their new bedroom. Later my mother arrived and stayed for a few days to help us recover from our forty-eight-hour journey.

A year after our return to the UK we were granted a British adoption order for both children in our local county court. Our social worker, despite our forebodings, was a very kind and helpful man, who gave us a glowing court report. The judge, too, was warm and friendly at the hearing. He also made a point of saying how impressed he was with the high standard of our Salvadorean adoption documents. Both children are now UK citizens in their own right.

They have been with us now for two years and are our greatest source of joy. Watching them both grow and develop is a never-ending pleasure and privilege. Benedict is a very handsome and macho toddler and, like many of his former countrymen, obsessed with football! He is a very big personality and hugely affectionate and loving. He also has a temper that is as volatile as any Central American volcano when he does not get his own way. He had suspected TB, but after a year as an outpatient at the London Chest Hospital has been pronounced fit. It is a dreadful thought to imagine what would have become of him in his native land where his TB would almost certainly have remained undetected until it was too late.

Veronica has shown none of the trauma we had previously anticipated when thinking about adopting a toddler. She is a bright, loving and very beautiful little girl adored by all who know her. The only lasting effect of her two years as a Salvadorean campesina is an obsession with food. She can pick a chicken leg absolutely clean and looks at every bit of food put in front of her with an adoring eye.

Her English was fluent in six weeks and she grew six inches in her first year with us. She never ceases to amaze us with her wisdom, humour and intelligence. We have explained her adoption to her many times and she likes looking at picture books from El Salvador with us. She is very proud of her brown skin and says, 'poor Mummy, you are a yellow and pink colour', adding that she and Benedict are brown and lovely! She attends our local Catholic nursery school where there are children from many different backgrounds, so she will never stand out because of her colour. Her friends are equally divided between white and ethnic and she is at ease with both.

In addition, we belong to several organizations for people who have adopted from abroad and we attend around four large gatherings a year for ICA families. Thus both our children know and are friends with plenty of children from El Salvador and other Third World countries. We hope this contact will help them to feel that they are not 'different' or 'unusual' in having been adopted from abroad. We want them both to grow up to be proud of their background and to be knowledgeable about their original culture. At present we expose them to positive elements of Salvadorean and Latin American life – music, pictures, books, food, fiestas, exhibitions and so forth – so that they will grow up with a basic understanding of El Salvador. This will, we hope, give them a clear sense of their own identity and self-worth as well as equip them to deal with any prejudice they may encounter.

They are, however, going to grow up in British society and we must give them the space and freedom to make their own choices of identity and lifestyle. We have to aim to strike the right balance – too much cultural input could result in overkill and total rejection of their origins, whilst too little cultural input could result in feelings of confusion about their identity. We want to avoid both of these scenarios. Neither of us feels particularly nationalistic and we hope that our children too will grow up with an international outlook and will respect, as we try to do, all cultures, races and creeds.

Above all, we realize that whatever we try to do they are free individuals who will ultimately decide their place in this world for themselves. We love them both so much, but know that our love must always be guided by this principle. We are giving them the opportunity to grow up free from the oppression of poverty, war and disease, and still cannot believe how lucky we are.

So this is the story of how we came to share our lives with these two extraordinary and beautiful children. The whole process was fraught with uncertainty from start to finish – it could have gone wrong at any stage, meaning that we would not now have our children. Moreover, since our return Marta has been forced to stop her adoption work due to the worsening situation in El Salvador. We were the second to last couple to get children adopted and back to the UK. So whatever the future may hold for us we shall always have ample reason to count our blessings – both of them!

2   Two little jungle flowers

Robert and Maureen Checketts

The following account differs from the rest of the series in deriving from a personal interview with the couple at their home in the West Country. They have not had the benefit of the higher education that most of our other contributors have received, and preferred to give us a verbal account of their experience. A visit was therefore arranged towards the end of the data-collecting period, after we had become familiar with some of the variations on the theme of inter-country adoption. They made us most welcome amid the pressing claims of their rich family life, and we are grateful to them for allowing us to intrude. Their story is all the more remarkable in showing what could be achieved with limited resources, given the necessary determination.

Robert and Maureen have two little girls from Sri Lanka, both of whom were adopted in early infancy: Chamila, who is now aged four (born 27 August, 1986 weighing 3lb 6oz), and Natasha aged three years (born 23 April, 1987 at a more normal weight). Thus the age gap of barely eight months is less than would be expected in an ordinary family, and possibly too close for comfort in the early stages of parenthood. However, the couple were anxious to make up for lost time; nothing daunted, they had even contemplated a third child from the same source until finally dissuaded by the realities of their bank account. And so, for the time being at least, their family is completed by two golden retrievers, a Jack Russell and two assertive cockatiels.

They married in 1972 when he was twenty-three and she was eighteen. Unusually they had known from the start of their relationship that their marriage was destined to remain childless, as Maureen had undergone a hysterectomy at the cruelly early age of seventeen. At first they lived in a flat above a shop, and when they first enquired about adoption after only a token period of marriage they were dismissed as too young. Prudently they waited ten years before re-applying, having meanwhile saved hard from their joint income to buy a house. Ironically, the immediate outcome of being vetted by the local Social Services department was further rejection on the grounds that Robert was now too old for a baby to be placed with them! This was particularly upsetting, as their approaches to a number of adoption societies had been equally fruitless. Nevertheless, they could be approved as potential adopters by the Social Services department if they were willing to consider children with 'special needs'.

Like so many women in today's adoption famine, Maureen had set her heart on a baby and could not easily reconcile herself to the prospect of an older child, least of all one with a medical handicap or a long history of social deprivation. Their sympathetic social worker came to their rescue and set the ball rolling for them to adopt a child from overseas. Through NAC they had been in touch with a woman who had managed to acquire a baby from Thailand and advised them to look into this possibility for themselves. With the other woman's encouragement they went ahead with this plan, and having decided that they would prefer a boy in the first instance they prepared a room for Jeremy, which was a name that particularly appealed to them even if it did not suggest a native of Bangkok. However, it was at this stage that their luck appeared to run out. Their social worker took early retirement (under some pressure), and her youthful successor arrived on their doorstep to inform them of a change of policy whereby they could no longer be supported in their efforts to adopt from abroad. What should they do, in that case? They might just as well get used to the idea that they were going to remain childless after all.

The couple were heart-broken, and Maureen especially felt compelled to sit down immediately and write long, emotional letters to both NAC and PPIAS (Parent to Parent Information on Adoption Services). As already implied she is not normally the most fluent of correspondents, but on this occasion her pen almost took on a life of its own. She was sent information on adoption procedures in a number of Third World countries. She and Robert then composed a letter which they despatched far and wide.

It so happened that their first response was from Sri Lanka, and they were hot on the trail. The year was 1986. They flew out to Colombo in September and returned with a baby four weeks later. After fourteen years of waiting the whole business took just twelve weeks! (Last year they heard again from their Social Services department who now wanted to help them, but they were happy to let them know that officialdom had been well and truly overtaken by private enterprise.)

This momentous event had occurred almost exactly four years before our visit. A private home study had been required, and the Sri Lankan authorities needed a letter stating why Maureen could not have children. Through NAC they obtained a list of other couples who had adopted Sri Lankan children and were able to contact several, who filled in details of cost and procedure for their benefit. An unexpected bonus was that legal and administrative fees were about a third of those in South American countries, and moreover there was no language barrier as everything was conducted in English. Since Sri Lanka is part of the British Commonwealth, adoption there is acceptable in this country, so it was merely a question of applying for British citizenship on behalf of any child they might import. The British Embassy in Colombo provided entry permits, and by a stroke of luck their Sri Lankan lawyer ran a travel agency on the side which was able to take care of all the practical arrangements. For a couple who had not travelled widely, this was welcome proof that fortune can indeed favour the brave, if not always consistently or predictably. There are other couples in our series who could be forgiven for envying them.

Robert and Maureen enjoyed their first trip to the Far East, and they had ample time to explore the island and admire the scenery. They lived comfortably for the most part, apart from the inevitable stomach bugs, and ate well. Admittedly Maureen was more suspicious of the local fare than Robert, yet she suffered no obvious ill-effects. Doubtless they were more than ready to return home with their precious bundle when the time came.

All went well on the home front, but any idea of accommodating to belated parenthood in a leisurely fashion was cut short by the rapidly worsening political situation in Sri Lanka. This was something that Robert and Maureen had not taken into account in their family planning, and they might well have been glad of a longer breathing space with their precious first child. But, having taken a few soundings, they reckoned it would have been risky to delay any longer than they did in case of losing the opportunity, so off they went again in pursuit of a second adoptee. This time they had intended that Robert would be accompanied by his mother in order that Maureen could remain at home to look after Chamila and the menagerie. Four days before they were due to board the aircraft, word came through that this arrangement was unacceptable to the Sri Lankan authorities, so it was Maureen who went, leaving her mother-in-law in charge at home. As on the previous occasion, they met the baby and her mother in the lawyer's office on their first day in Sri Lanka, when papers were signed and the probationary period could begin. And once again they were obliged to make their own amusements for the necessary four weeks, this time without the advantage of novelty. They had no further glimpse of either baby until the court hearing, when it was handed over together with the adoption certificate. Robert told us that Chamila's mother thrust a dirty bottle at him, and the baby at Maureen, before rushing out of the court without so much as a backward glance. In Natasha's case the mother sat breastfeeding the baby throughout the hearing, then handed her over and stood there crying. They had been warned by other adopters that this might happen but still found it extremely upsetting. Plainly, inter-country adoption is not for the incurably soft-hearted.

The cost of adopting a second child proved somewhat heavier for the couple (although of course no money changed hands for the babies themselves), as Maureen had by now stopped earning. In the first fourteen years of her marriage she had worked for a firm of solicitors, initially as a cleaner but ending as their housekeeper. Robert continues to work as a stonemason for the local council and is currently in charge of a gang of kerb-layers. Meanwhile the couple have always taken a pride in their home which their two little 'jungle flowers' have done much to enrich. Even before the children arrived, their dogs could be relied upon to counteract the sterile atmosphere of some childless homes; for those whose prime purpose, at a certain stage of life, is to care for dependent creatures and nurture them towards a state of maturity, animals are not enough.

Chamila was seven weeks old at adoption, Natasha only four weeks. Neither child has caused any undue concern for their health or development to date, although the older one – who is now almost ready for school – appears to be the brighter of the two. The younger one's progress has been generally somewhat slower, perhaps because she enjoys being the baby of the family albeit by a small margin. In our presence the children were lively and at times demanding. A system was evolved whereby one parent remained in the fairly spacious garden with all five younger members of the family, whilst the other fielded our questions in the equally spacious lounge/dining room, taking it in turns to hold the floor. This way it did not take too long to absorb the essential features of their story, which on a weekend visit might otherwise have proved elusive.

Despite their original preference for a boy the couple were only too pleased to settle for a second girl, partly for the sake of companionship but also for practical reasons (e.g. sleeping arrangements in time to come). We were not absolutely convinced that they had finally given up all hope of a third child, but meanwhile they have plenty to keep them occupied. Interestingly, they have got to know some thirty other couples who have adopted from overseas, and periodically they attend grand reunions. This spirit of camaraderie is quite likely to be typical of those who venture abroad for their children, and NAC has been active in promoting it. They know at least four other local couples with children from Sri Lanka, and have remained in touch with a fifth couple in the home counties who flew out on the same plane when they adopted Chamila. If there was ever a time when either partner had any misgivings over the wisdom of inter-country adoption, these have long since vanished. However, it is almost unknown for *any* adoptive parents to experience second thoughts about their decision, regardless of the obstacles they have had to overcome or the subsequent anxieties with which they may have had to contend. As a human enterprise adoption tends to speak for itself; it is involuntary childlessness that can lead to permanent heartache.

To end on a cautionary note, not all of us are well equipped to rear other people's children, especially when born of an alien culture. Thus there will always be some in positions of authority who for whatever reason 'don't hold with' inter-country adoption. Let them keep their opinions to themselves, for by the same token there will always be others – neither rebels at heart nor peculiarly adept at 'working the system' – who are bent on circumventing bureaucracy if they can. Such is certainly true of this resolute couple, who are also lucky enough to live in a multi-racial area. What they have achieved is unusual by any standards, yet unlikely to attract untoward attention in their neighbourhood.

3 Columbia to the rescue

Elizabeth and Simon Day

Simon and Elizabeth live in a small village called Hunton, about five miles from Maidstone in Kent. They were married in 1976 when they were both in their early thirties. Elizabeth tells their story.

Simon comes from an old-established farming family and has lived in Kent all his life. He has an elder brother, Robert, and he and his wife Sarah live and farm three miles away with their two grown-up daughters. Simon's sister Diana also lives nearby with her 14-year-old twins.

My family history is slightly more complicated, in that I have moved around rather more than Simon. My father was a senior naval officer until invalided out of the Royal Navy in 1956 when he took up farming. I have an elder sister, Anne, who is married to an Australian and living near Melbourne with their 14-year-old son, and my younger brother John is married with two sons and living in Canada, so we are well spread out. John was going to be our first stepping-stone to adopting a baby from Columbia, although he did not realize this at the time.

We had the usual 'years of trying' which will be familiar to many people, with still more years of fertility tests. When we realized that it was going to be very unlikely that we would ever have a child of our own we applied to Kent County Council (KCC) to go on their adoption list. We never had a visit from them but received a standard letter listing several reasons why a couple may not be eligible to adopt a baby. The only reason we could see which might apply to us was my age, as I was then 36 years old. We thought that perhaps someone should have come to see us and at least explained it to us and seen whether or not we were suitable, as we did receive another letter later on asking us whether we would like to consider a 'hard to place' child. We were obviously not too old for this.

Simon and I then tried to explore the possibilities of adopting from abroad but we had no idea how to go about this. The National Association for the Childless (NAC) gave us the address of Parent to Parent Information Advisory Service (PPIAS) and they gave us addresses of orphanages around the world. At that time Manila sounded the most likely place but they required a home study report done by a qualified social worker and KCC refused. We liked the idea of helping the Vietnamese but this too proved difficult.

Some very good friends of ours had a brother-in-law in the diplomatic service and they said they would write to a contact they had in Brazil. Almost immediately we were told of twin white babies wanting parents! This was just too good to be true and we frantically started collecting all the necessary papers together, in particular the home study report which we now knew was essential for whichever country we adopted from. PPIAS were very helpful over this and put us in touch with a social worker in Essex who was prepared to do private home studies. Unfortunately, before we even had an appointment with the social worker, one of the twins had died and the other was found to have a heart defect; all very sad. However, it had made us realize that there were a lot of papers to obtain and a lot of patience needed. We had the home study done in May 1982 and asked three friends to write references for us, at the same time realizing how difficult it would be for them to know what sort of parents we might make at some possible date in the future! The most amusing document was a psychiatrist's report, for the poor man did not really know how to go about it. As he said, his patients usually came to him to be cured, not to be certified sane! I think he may have anticipated that we would be back by the time we had finished, but six-and-a-half years later we still have not required his treatment. At this time there were various trips to London to get copies of birth certificates, the marriage certificate, and so on.

We had just done all this when our contact in Brazil left the diplomatic service and none of our letters were answered. The Falklands war did not help matters either.

At about this time we had Giles, a student friend of my brother's from Canada, staying for the summer, and he cheered us up no end. Giles' parents, Pat and Tony, also visited us in May and we mentioned our longing for a baby, and as it turned out it was lucky we did. Simon had cracked a rib playing cricket just before Giles arrived so things were not good. However, Giles helped on the farm and stood in for Simon on the cricket field. It was on one of these occasions while we were watching cricket that we told Pat and Tony of our troubles and how we wanted to adopt a baby from abroad, but it was not proving very easy. After a few minutes, and I can remember the moment as if it were yesterday, Pat said, 'I think I can help you'. She must have said it with such conviction that we believed her, although we still had reservations as to how this lovely lady whom we had only just met could possibly help us. It transpired that Tony had met, through his business in Bogota, a lawyer by the name of Jorgé Cardenas, and over the years Tony and Pat had become very good friends of Jorgé and his wife Cecelia and their family. We learned that Jorgé had been one of the original benefactors of the orphanage FANA (Fundacion para la Adopcion la Ninez Abandonada) and knew one of the ladies working there, a Betty del Castillo.

Tony and Pat were due to return to Canada shortly but promised to write to Jorgé and to keep us in touch with what happened. This was going to be fairly easy, as I had already planned to go to Canada in June to see my brother. My mother had died the previous November and I had had so much to do settling her estate and selling her house that Simon thought a break would do me good. Unfortunately, being a farmer he could not leave the farm in the summer. By the time I arrived in Toronto, Pat had received a letter from Jorgé Cardenas telling us to ring Betty del Castillo who was, at that time, holidaying in New York (could I really ring someone I didn't know while they were on holiday?). I did, and she kindly told me then and there what documents we would need but to write in the first instance to the orphanage for an application form with a covering letter giving a brief account of ourselves. This was fairly easy; having written to so many people already we knew who we were quite well.

What a holiday I was having. John entertained me very well; he had just bought a house on the outskirts of Toronto and was in the process of persuading a childhood sweetheart to return from South Africa and marry him. All this was very romantic, and it certainly helped me to have something else to think about. John and I have always been very close, and in our attempt to adopt a baby he was very supportive. At the end of my ten-day holiday, I went home to Simon and we waited eagerly for the application form to arrive, which it did eventually at the end of July via Pat in Toronto from Jorgé in Bogota, Colombia. We really had some work to do then to get our documents together and have them notarized, authenticated etc., all of which was very new to us. The staff at the Colombian Consulate in London were helpful here and told us exactly what was required and which papers needed signing and by whom.

We had to have all of the following: three personal references stating honourability and good conduct of prospective adoptive parents, which had to be taken by the friends concerned to a Public Notary; one bank reference and an accountant's return signed by a solicitor; and certified copies of birth and marriage certificates which had to be taken to the legalization section of the Foreign and Commonwealth Office in London. These trips to London were becoming quite costly at £3 per document every time it was stamped, and then everything had to be taken to the Colombian Consulate in London, as all documents, references, medicals etc., regardless of how many stamps they already had, needed to be authenticated. This process took twenty-four hours (two journeys to London!) and nearly £9 per document. Never mind, we knew it was going to be worth it in the end. All this was a pretty hectic time, but at least we were doing something constructive. Then things started to go wrong. We heard from Jorgé Cardenas that FANA would not accept a home study report unless it was done by a social worker attached to a Social Services Department. This threw us into a turmoil, as the lady who did our report for us lived and worked in Essex and was not employed by KCC, and KCC would not do one on us. However, the lady agreed to write a covering letter outlining her status and employment qualifications, get it notarized and so on, and we hoped that this would do.

By 31 August all our documents were ready and on Jorgé Cardenas' advice we sent them to him with a covering letter to the director of FANA.

This time there was nothing we could do except wait. We wished we could start proceedings for an entry visa for our baby to come into this country, but you cannot do so until you have a named child.

On 25 September we had a letter, not from the orphanage but from Jorgé, enclosing a letter to him from Mercedes de Martinez, the director of FANA. Briefly, the letter stated that our laws were not compatible with Colombian law, inasmuch as Britain does not recognize the legality of Colombian adoption or look upon it as final even after it has gone through Colombian courts. Their worry was that we could adopt a baby under Colombian law but possibly get turned down by a British court, thus rendering the child stateless and putting the paternity in limbo. We wrote to the Home Office for clarification of the law but did not receive a reply for two weeks, and even then it was not very helpful. However, they said they would write to FANA explaining our laws to them. An official did this at the end of November, stressing that because the UK does not recognize Colombian adoption, there had to be an absolute assurance that the couple concerned would be able to complete the adoption procedures, and all these checks had to be done before the Home Office would grant an entry visa for the child to come into the country. After this there was complete silence from FANA, and when we telephoned Jorgé on 9 December he promised to chase it up but he was going to be away for three weeks. That was not a very happy Christmas for us. We tried telephoning FANA but Mrs de Martinez was always out or away, to add to our frustration. It was 26 January before we were able to speak with Jorgé. He had also been trying to get hold of someone at FANA and told us to ring him back in a couple of days, by which time he hoped to have an answer for us. Jorgé was surprised that nothing had been resolved and told us to send him all the relevant papers from the Home Office and FANA. In that letter to him we did ask whether we might be better off trying another orphanage in Colombia.

Our friend in the Foreign Office at this time offered to contact the British Ambassador in Bogota. Yes please, we said, we need all the help we can get. What we really wanted to know was whether FANA was still considering our case or not; we just felt we were being ignored.

There were so many kind people helping us that we just kept going so as not to let them down, but there were times when we wondered whether we were doing the right thing – surely if we *were* right it would not be so enormously difficult. We did feel we had prevailed upon Jorgé Cardenas' kindness for too long; after all, he was only a friend of a friend and his firm were corporate lawyers, not family welfare lawyers, but whenever we mentioned any of this he assured us that he was only too glad to help.

Three weeks later we received a letter from Jorgé in which he pointed out that the Home Office directive does not state that British law requires the completion of the adoption proceedings in Colombia in order to grant an entry visa, because an adoption made in Colombia has no validity in Britain. Our own authorities go through very lengthy procedures when a request is made for an entry visa, to make reasonably sure that the adoption will go through in their country. The entry visa is not granted until this is done. Jorgé said he would write to FANA with his suggestions and interpretations of the law in order that their lawyer could decide whether his suggestions were feasible. He sent us a copy of his letter to FANA which was fairly forceful. This man sure is on our side and yet we haven't even met him!

Another three weeks later, we received another letter from Jorgé informing us that he had received a letter from the British Vice Consul, who had stepped in to give information to the Colombian authorities and to FANA about adoption matters in England. Before we could adequately express our gratitude to this kind lady she was promoted to another post in Canada. However, she had written some rather lengthy notes on adopting a baby from Colombia as she helped another couple from England to adopt a baby from an orphanage outside Bogota. This information was encouraging, as it did prove that the Colombian and British courts could reconcile their differences.

Friday, 25 March 1983 was a red letter day for us, as we received a letter from Mrs Mercedes de Martinez herself, informing us that they were now fully aware of the laws governing adoption in the UK and therefore saw it as feasible to make a placement with us. What a relief! We were very excited but cautious, as things had gone wrong before and we still had no idea how long we would have to wait. Mrs de Martinez had enclosed a FANA contract, a list of documents required and three copies of a Power of Attorney for them to appoint a lawyer to act on our behalf in Colombia *once we had been offered a child*. Seeing those words on paper was quite amazing. Mrs de Martinez also said in her letter that the recommendation by Jorgé Cardenas meant a lot to them. We really do have much to thank him for.

Of course all our documents were ready, but when we read through the list we were horrified to note that all the documents had to be dated less than two months prior to submission, which meant two more trips to London and another set of rubber stamps on everything and two more medicals for Simon and myself. We were extremely lucky to have an obliging GP who did this for us. The update on the psychiatrist's report was slightly more worrying – how could we possibly still be in good mental health? Our documents went to FANA by express delivery on 5 April and we just hoped we wouldn't have to wait three years for a baby, as we had heard it could be that long on the waiting list.

Our friends and relatives were all very supportive during this time and I know they wished us every success, but apart from a few really close friends it was difficult for them to grasp what was going on. It was all so complicated that even Simon and I had difficulty in understanding some of it, let alone explaining it to anyone else. However, it was great knowing that everyone was behind us. We had also had a letter from the new Vice Consul in Bogota, who promised to help in any way he could and looked forward to seeing us there. We hoped he would not suffer the same kind of transplant as his predecessor before we could get to Bogota.

On 16 April we had a telegram from FANA asking us to telephone them. Oh dear, we thought, what could have gone wrong now? When we phoned them there was no reply from the office as it was a public holiday, so we had to wait until the next day. Eventually, we got through and were told we had a baby boy! It was quite unbelievable and neither of us was really prepared for it. Mrs de Martinez was giving us a few details which we managed to write down; we did not know whether to laugh or cry and even now when I think of those words it brings tears to my eyes. Our baby was called Hugo Osorio and he was born on 11 April. I think they gave us his weight and length, but at the time those details were quite irrelevant. What joy that phone call gave us, although we could hardly believe it was real. The telephone was red hot that day, telling everyone our good news; we even phoned Canada and Australia at the first opportunity. It was so soon after we had been accepted. Maybe FANA just got tired of all the legal wrangles. We certainly did but all that was behind us now. Or so we thought.

After about two weeks we received a letter from FANA enclosing a photograph of Hugo. He looked a gorgeous baby even on a one-inch square print! They also sent a copy of Hugo's birth certificate and the release form signed by his mother the day he was born. FANA told us that the legal procedures in Colombia took about six to eight weeks and there would be no point in going out there until then, we must just be patient. In the meantime we had to apply for Hugo's entry visa from the Home Office to bring him into the country. We had by this time decided to keep the name Hugo; we liked it and it seemed unlucky to change it. Our next job was to get the documents that FANA had sent translated into English and taken to the Home Office with the treasured home study report. That trip involved hours of waiting and then we were told they were incomplete. The medical certificate for Hugo was not detailed enough and, worse still, our adoption laws require the child's mother to sign a release form at least six weeks *after* the baby is born. We were told that if the orphanage signed a declaration that all efforts to find the mother had been made without success then the child is said to be abandoned. This seemed quite awful to us, as Hugo's mother was an unmarried student who had gone to FANA so that her baby could be legally adopted and in no way did she abandon him. However, there was not much we could do about it.

We now found out that the DHSS who were to report to the Home Office on our case would not accept a private home study. It had to be done by the KCC before an entry visa would be issued. It was two weeks before one of us managed to speak to the social worker in charge of the adoption and then we were told that there was no way they could start checks on us until they had a letter from the Home

Office stating that they had all the child's documents, but she did say that once they were given the go-ahead the checks would not take very long.

On 3 June we had a call from FANA to say that the Colombian courts were ready and we could go and collect Hugo. What frustration: no joy from the KCC, and the Home Office told us they had instructed the DHSS and thence the KCC that all was in order three weeks before this, so that they could have started the check three weeks ago. There was a lot of anger on our part, but I think it fell on deaf ears.

Our social worker, Mrs H, was extremely evasive and when we eventually got to speak to her on 7 June she told us that they would have to do six two-hour interviews, see all our financial statements and interview our referees. Mrs H had written to our previous social worker for permission to use her home study, but alas she was on holiday for two weeks, so more delay. We could see no reason why her permission had to be obtained as we had paid for the document, so surely it was ours to use as we chose? Mrs H then said she had no idea when she would be able to start these interviews as they were very busy and she was going on holiday. She thought maybe she could manage October – unbelievable! We could visualize Hugo drawing his pension before we were able to collect him and this was after the same Mrs H had told us in April that the checks would not take long to do. Two days later we were told that the DHSS were indeed insisting on a full report and as they were short-staffed they were referring it to another department for reallocation.

In desperation we phoned the DHSS in London and spoke to a very helpful girl, who was fairly sure that nobody had instructed Kent Social Services to do a full report but only a statutory one as we had already gathered all the relevant documents together including the home study. That same day we heard that an uncle of Simon's knew one of the senior men at KCC – not in the Social Services Department, but any straw is better than none, and we immediately telephoned him with a complete dossier of our complaints. We were very determined by this time that nothing was going to stop us going out to collect Hugo, so if we upset a few people on the way it was a pity but unavoidable.

Two days later (10 June) we had a call from Mrs H, who made an appointment to come and see us the next day, a Saturday. I think we must have pressed the right button because not only had we got an appointment but it was the first time in all these months that anyone at the Social Services Department had returned our call.

The next day arrived and so did Mrs H. We were surprised at how sympathetic she appeared and she told us that she would only be doing a shortened report, since the home study report we had had done by the private social worker was perfectly acceptable. But Mrs H did say that it was unlikely that her report would be finished before August owing to her holiday, pressure of work, etc. By this time we were worried that FANA would just get fed up with the whole thing and give our dear Hugo to someone else.

Meanwhile, we had heard of another couple who had adopted from Colombia and we rang them to see if they had waited for their entry visa before collecting their baby as we knew that people had done this from other countries. They did, in fact, go to Colombia before their baby's visa was ready but they had not been allowed to take the baby out of the country until the Colombian authorities were certain that the child would be allowed into Britain. It made sense but it was all very frustrating. We knew that we would just have to keep badgering those who were preventing us from collecting our baby until they let us go.

Simon telephoned the British Embassy in Bogota and spoke to an official who promised to put FANA in the picture, and we promised to be there soon. Ten days later Simon managed to get hold of Mrs H after a great deal of difficulty, and she told him that all the documents were in order and had been passed to her superior. Part of the delay had been due to Mrs H writing to the NSPCC, the probation office and the police to make sure that we were not on their books. Perhaps all prospective mothers should have these checks done on them before having children? If only Mrs H and all the others could have kept us in the picture, but we were never told what was going on.

Every day either Simon or I rang the DHSS to see if our documents had arrived and eventually on 27 June we were told that they had. A call to the Home Office told us that everything was in order and Hugo had his entry visa to come into this country. Wonderful! We had had our inoculations and thank goodness they were not out of date, and we were able to book on the next available flight to Bogota – 15 July, my mother's birthday. Two tickets out and three back: what a lovely thought that was. That same day we wrote and telephoned FANA and the British Consul in Bogota, Jorgé Cardenas, Maureen Robson (the Ambassador's wife) and Pat and Tony Fenn who started it all. FANA had offered to find accommodation for us with friends of Mercedes which we readily accepted.

Hugo was now 4,320 g (9½ lbs) and even though we still had not seen him we were really beginning to think of him as our baby. The next two weeks were full, and although there was plenty to do the time went very slowly. We had to make all sorts of complicated arrangements with the bank, as the British Enbassy had advised us not to take any money out even in travellers' cheques due to the appalling security. We had no idea how much money we would need for lawyers' fees, translations, etc., to say nothing of our accommodation and food for two weeks.

There was also the matter of finishing off Hugo's bedroom and lots of little things to buy. Our family and friends were wonderful and were very excited for us. My only regret was that neither of my parents were with us to share in our joy, especially my Mum who had so wanted a grandchild that she could watch grow up in this country. Even my brother and sister were rather a long way away, but they telephoned constantly which was good.

Friday 15 July finally dawned and we left home at 6.45 a.m. to be driven to Gatwick by a good friend. We took off at 10.30 a.m. and arrived in Bogota after two stops at 4.45 a.m. local time. We were met by a taxi-driver called Lewis who got us through passport control and took us to our digs. Lewis was to be our driver throughout our stay. He could speak a bit of English which was handy, as our Spanish was almost non-existent in spite of trying to learn it from cassettes before coming out. Once at our digs our landlady told us we could not see our baby until Monday (more frustrations) so we had Saturday and Sunday to occupy ourselves. Taxi-driver Lewis stepped in here and took us to the gold museum. What a place: really interesting, all about the Colombian Indians, their gold figures, plates, jewelry, etc. So much wealth shut up in a vault when outside there were children begging! Lewis then took us for a drive around Bogota, which was again full of contrasts. Every time we saw children playing in the streets, we wondered if our Hugo looked like them. In the afternoon we went for a walk, trying desperately to use up some time. We did some window-shopping and bought two apples and two oranges for £6 (if our calculations were correct!). Our digs were going to cost £43 a day for bed and breakfast which we thought was quite a lot, but as it turned out our landlady was a great help with Hugo even if her cooking did leave a lot to be desired. However, the following day (Sunday) we had been invited to lunch at the British Embassy by John and Maureen Robson who were friends of friends of ours in Kent. Unfortunately I had a minor stomach upset which we thought might be a touch of food poisoning from a local hamburger the day before and we just hoped it wouldn't get worse. We had a lovely day with the Robsons, a nice English lunch and a drive through the countryside surrounding Bogota. This was lovely, very beautiful and green as

Bogota stands high up on a plateau. We drove back to Bogota through the shanty towns and were again exposed to dreadful poverty, the people just living in shelters on the hillside, but the children we saw running about looked very healthy and well fed and, best of all, they looked happy. We wondered whether most of the children in the orphanages came from these homes but Maureen pointed out that these families were intensely proud and loyal and would always take in orphans from other members of their families. It was from the better-off families who would disown an unmarried mother that the children usually came. Obviously there were many exceptions but there were too many unwanted children.

We returned to our digs after tea and I went to bed determined to be fit the next day. I don't think either Simon or I slept much that night, the excitement of seeing our baby next day was too much.

Monday, 18 July 1983. We arrived at FANA at 9 a.m. as instructed. There were several other couples there, mainly from the United States, but there was one couple from Holland. One of the nurses came into the sitting room, sat down next to us and told us that she had some bad news. We must have looked suddenly pale because she very quickly told us it was nothing to worry about, Hugo had a slight chest infection but they hoped he would be fit enough to travel (they hoped!). It had never crossed our minds that the poor little chap might be ill. We handed the nurse the clothes we had brought with us including a lovely shawl my mother had knitted – she had known that one day we would have a baby. More waiting, about fifteen minutes, and then the same nurse appeared with Hugo. He was quite the most beautiful baby we had ever seen and he was ours. This was hard to believe, but when Simon and I held him for the first time it felt absolutely right, as though he belonged, which of course he did. We can remember that moment as if it were yesterday but it is hard to describe our feelings: great happiness, immense gratitude, and wonder that this beautiful little bundle was now part of our family and would be for ever. The nuns and nurses were very kind and were obviously very pleased to see us. We were given full instructions on Hugo's diet and medication and strict orders to contact their doctor if we were worried about him.

We returned to our digs, where Simon left us as he had to go to the bank, the lawyer and the British Consul. Poor Simon had a dreadful time at the bank. No one on the front desk could speak English and it was a while before he could get beyond the front desk to the Manager who could do so. However, he finally succeeded and we had some money. Next stop was Mr Carter at the British Consulate, where it became obvious that he had done sterling work on our behalf. Most importantly, Simon was able to telex home with news of our son. Simon also had to visit our appointed lawyer, a Mr Gomez, to collect Hugo's Colombian passport and visa. We had thought that we would have to get the passport done including all the photographs, translations, etc. but obviously someone had gone to a great deal of trouble on our behalf and it then became clear that we would be able to leave Bogota within a week, instead of a fortnight. We had to ask the British Caledonian office if they could change the tickets but they said they would not know until the next day.

In the meantime, back at our digs, I was learning all about Hugo with the landlady's help. Having never changed a nappy or fed a baby, I needed all the help I could get. Hugo's chest was rather wheezy but the landlady thought it was all right. I cannot say that those first few days were bliss, as I was too worried that we were not doing it right to really enjoy Hugo and we wanted him to sleep as much as possible so he would get better, so we didn't even cuddle him very much.

The next day we had been told to go back to the orphanage to see around it. We left Hugo with our landlady as the air was quite cool, and we had been advised that because of his chest it would be better to leave him. FANA is not a particularly large orphanage. There were about 130 children from babies up to 11-year-olds and a staff of eighty, and the place is run solely on donations without any help from the State at all. It had a very friendly atmosphere, but it was heart-rending to see so many children without homes to go to.

There was good news from British Caledonian Airways. They had space on their flight leaving that Friday, really wonderful. I had a bit of an adventure getting to the BCA office. We both left FANA in the taxi with Lewis driving and we went to the bank. In order to save time, and as the BCA offices were not far away, I said I would go in the taxi there, check on the flight and come back to the bank. Simon told Lewis to do this and we drove off. We hadn't gone far when I realized that we were going in the wrong direction. I told Lewis to stop but he would not; he just kept driving. I was getting frantic, having visions of being whisked away for ransom, or worse. Eventually, when nearly hysterical, I managed to get Lewis to stop and made myself understood that I wanted to go to the BCA office, which he did. Lewis had thought Simon had told him to take me home to the digs! I must have gained a few more grey hairs that day.

On Wednesday we had lunch again at the British Embassy, a grand occasion for Hugo's very first social outing. We also had tea with the Cardenas that day which we were really looking forward to. They had made all this possible, but sadly, after all the phone calls and correspondence with Jorgé, he was in the States on business. However, Cecelia and their large grown-up family were there and made us very welcome. Their house was like something out of a glossy magazine with beautiful furnishings. This was indeed another grand occasion, a beautiful house overlooking the city and with enough staff to make our brief stay very comfortable. The family made a great fuss of Hugo who behaved impeccably, sleeping most of the time. Two of Jorgé's and Cecelia's children had adopted children from FANA, so they knew what it was all about and perhaps this explained a little of why Jorgé did so much for us.

Simon describes the next day in the diary as being one of the worst! It started well with a trip to FANA for Hugo's check-up, and although he still had a slight infection the doctor pronounced him fit to travel. Simon left us at the digs and went back to the bank and British Consulate, where he rang his parents to tell them we would be on an earlier flight – a whole week early. While he was out I started to feel really ill and was very sick. Maureen Robson found an English-speaking doctor but we either had to go to his surgery or wait until the evening for a visit. We elected to go to the surgery since a quick cure was essential. I nearly passed out on the way and the diagnosis was a severe gastric infection with a temperature of 102°. The doctor said there was no way I could travel the next day and I should really be in hospital. However, he gave me pills and medicine and by the next morning I was feeling a lot better: amazing what determination can do! It was a bad night all round, as Hugo was awake most of the time too, so we were all pretty tired by the morning. However, our flight was not until 6 p.m. and as the day wore on we all felt better. Our one thought was to get on that flight and let everything else take care of itself.

By 4.30 p.m. we were ready and Lewis arrived to take us to the airport. He gave us a farewell gift of some coffee which was good of him, but he also presented us with a fairly hefty bill for his services! The airport was packed, and it took us a while to find the right departure lounge where we managed to get one seat between us. I had to feed and change Hugo which was no easy matter in the crowded space, but we managed and at 6.30 p.m. we were called to the flight and at last Simon and I and our dear son Hugo were on our way home. It was an uneventful flight, except that Hugo had a stomach upset too, but the crew were wonderful and very helpful. It was a great moment to land in England and be met by great friends of ours, the Mortons. We arrived home happy but exhausted and were given a grand welcome by

Simon's parents. Granny couldn't wait to give her new grandson a cuddle. It was so wonderful to be home that we felt nothing else could now go wrong, we had our darling baby and really nothing else mattered.

Hugo still wasn't feeding properly, but as he seemed happy and slept fairly well we were not too worried. Our health visitor was away so we did not see her for a week, but she immediately diagnosed Hugo's trouble: he was not sucking properly. She suggested that the reason was probably that in the orphanage they had very large holes in the teats to make feeding time easier and he had never learnt to suck properly. Once the poor little chap had mastered the art he was well away, but by this time he had lost a lot of weight and was down to under 7 lbs, partly due to our ignorance although his chest infection hadn't helped. Our health visitor was great and after a while Hugo was gaining weight. He has never looked back and we now have a job to stop him eating too much!

We were of course visited by social workers at very frequent intervals, which we could well have done without but had to put up with. The next step was to adopt Hugo through the British courts, and we wanted to do this as soon as possible. We contacted a solicitor who we had been told specialized in adoption cases and he agreed to help, although he had not handled a foreign one before. We handed over all the documents that we had collected *en route* and he prepared a 'statement of facts'. The only real stumbling-block was the fact that Hugo's natural mother could not be traced after six weeks to sign her agreement releasing her child for adoption. She had signed it the day after Hugo was born which Simon and I think is the more sensible and humane rule, but ours is not to reason why. In British law, the mother has to sign the release form at least six weeks *after* the birth, which gives her time to recover from the ordeal but also to change her mind. Luckily, the solicitor obtained signatures from FANA to say she could not be found, further documents proving that FANA was a licensed institute and yet other documents declaring that Hugo's mother had given FANA permission to have her child adopted. There were also documents and signatures confirming that the judge in Bogota who had made all these statements was qualified to do so. A so-called 'guardian *ad litem*' had been appointed by the probation office and he had to visit us, so for the next three months there was a lot of coming and going, some visitors more welcome than others. It was really wonderful to see all our friends and show off our handsome son, but we could really have done without the official visitors, as more than anything we wanted to be left alone to get on with our new life. Hugo was a delight to look after. He was very contented, smiled at everyone, and slept reasonably well at night: how lucky we were. Even our dog, Boots, whom we had had for four years, took to Hugo, or at least he didn't show any jealousy, which was what we had feared in view of his long reign as an 'only child'.

After numerous letters from our solicitors who had obviously done a great job for us, we were eventually told our case was to be heard in court on 30 November. Hugo was to be present too. Simon and I were extremely nervous, although we had been told that it was almost a formality as the judge would have already seen our papers, but we both had a feeling that something could go wrong. Happily all went well and Hugo was ours for ever, his name was now Hugo Day and he could have a British passport. What a tremendous sense of achievement. Judge Kee was a kindly man who told us he was most impressed by the way we had gathered all the documents together leaving nothing out (thanks to our solicitor, Richard Flower). He also commented that he was pleased we had stuck to the law and not taken any short cuts. He said it was a moving and remarkable story and hoped we would all three give each other the happiness we had striven for.

Having completed all the formalities we were, at last, able to concentrate on Hugo's christening, an event we had been keenly anticipating for a very long time. There were many friends and relations we wanted to invite, as well as people who had done so much to help us. Hugo was christened in Marden Parish Church on a Sunday in November. It was a very moving service. He behaved beautifully and looked adorable in a christening gown made in 1876 for his adoptive great-grandfather, which only just fitted as Hugo was by now 7 months old. Later that day he was guest of honour at a party given by Simon's parents.

SIX YEARS LATER

Hugo is still the happy soul he was as a baby. He has his bad moments like any other youngster, but he has given us so much pleasure and brought such happiness into our lives that all the problems we encountered were well worthwhile. He does well at school, seems extremely bright and gets on with other children. We have told him he is adopted and where he came from and how special he is, but we don't labour the point, as at 6½ years old he doesn't want to be too different from his friends. We do know one or two other children who are adopted and I think this helps.

We never went back for another baby, although when we were in

Colombia this was our original intention. As time went on and we had settled in with Hugo the thought of uprooting our lives and Hugo's and starting all over again seemed too much; I was over 40 and somehow we kept putting it off. We have no regrets and hope Hugo doesn't later. Certainly at the moment he has never asked for a brother or sister and we can do more with him than some of our friends with two or three children. He plays well on his own and he has many friends of his own age nearby.

To anyone contemplating adopting a baby from overseas we would say yes, every time, but you must have determination, and we were very lucky to have so many kind people helping us to make our dream come true.

4   Aeroplanes and epidurals

Susan and Wally Freeman

Susie and Wally Freeman adopted their son Thomas from Brazil. They brought him to England when he was 5 weeks old. Eleven months later their daughter Lucy was born to them. These are their recollections.

SUSIE'S STORY

My miscarriages were all very badly timed. The first was on the way back from honeymoon in St Lucia. I was wearing a pair of light yellow trousers. We had checked all our luggage through and then the incoming flight ran off the end of the runway and ended up in the jungle. Not a sanitary towel to be had in St Lucia airport! We were there all night and the only thing that the airport staff could offer was a baby's nappy.

The second miscarriage arrived on the very day that the builder had removed the upstairs lavatory from the house we had just moved into in East Sheen. Wally was away, but the builder was very kind – having six children of his own he seemed to be quite used to this sort of thing.

The third miscarriage arrived two days before we went to Brazil to pick up Thomas.

We were married in 1982, both well into our thirties. I had travelled all over the world – as a dancer when I was younger and then as an actress. I was ready to start a family. Wally had an unsuccessful marriage behind him (and without children) so we decided to try straight away. Well, it didn't happen as we had planned. I don't think there was any particular reason. I believe that fertility for some people gets less as they get older and I was one of those people. We were convinced that I would have a successful pregnancy eventually, but time was running out and we wanted a baby.

I think a woman's desire for a baby is very strong, especially when you know that you've only a few more breeding years left. I was very determined, and the more obstacles that came my way, the more determined I became. Wally thought that I was quite mad during this time, likening me to Pam in the television series *Dallas* who was obsessed with having a baby. He didn't know anyone who had adopted a baby from abroad and therefore didn't believe that it was possible. I put his attitude down to the fact that he was working for IBM at the time. Anyone who knows anything about large corporations will know that employees go to work every day in a dark grey suit, crisp white shirt and dark tie. Wally has since started his own business with some colleagues and they now wear sports jackets, slacks and hush puppies – quite way out! The breakthrough came, however, when he went to a university reunion and met an old friend of his who had adopted a child from abroad. This convinced him that it was indeed possible, so then we were off and running. We both believed that eventually I would conceive a baby of our own, but we decided to go for both routes. Oh, the blissful ignorance of well-rested, would-be parents!

The first step was to get all our papers together – home study reports, references, etc. These had to be translated and notarized. I made many trips to Somerset House, the Home Office, lawyers and various embassies in order to get everything in order.

A Sri Lankan friend of mine with whom I played badminton had heard of a baby in Sri Lanka waiting for adoption, but unfortunately we didn't have our papers ready in time. Another couple, Paul and Sheila Starr, had adopted a baby boy from Brazil and were very helpful to us. They put us in touch with a Mormon priest in Brazil who had found their baby for them. We sent off our papers to him and waited.

Neither Wally nor I speak Portuguese, but luckily my sister and brother-in-law, Sarah and Ben Box, are fluent in the language. Ben agreed to make midnight phone calls to Brazil to check on progress. We plied Ben with large whiskies to give him courage and Sarah took charge of the dictionary. We had three-way conversations. The priest in Brazil would say something to Ben, he would translate with the aid of Sarah and we would reply via the same route. One night we were asked if we would like twins. Again in blissful ignorance, we said 'yes'. However, they never materialized. Sadly, the priest in Brazil was unable to find us a baby so we eventually decided to try another route.

Sarah and Ben were in touch with a lecturer they had met at university, and he had a very good friend in Brazil called Jamir. Jamir and his wife Coletta changed our lives. They agreed to help us for no personal gain, only the desire to see a couple have a family and to help one of the thousands of abandoned children in Brazil. We sent them our papers and they put our name on an adoption list at the local maternity hospital. Again we waited.

At about this time I decided to take up ice-skating again, perhaps trying to regain lost youth. But, whatever the reason, it proved to be a mistake. I broke my ankle and was totally immobilized. I had to lie on the sofa all day. During this time, I became pregnant again.

One evening in January 1985 when Wally was away on a business trip, I had a phone call from Brazil. They had a new-born baby boy for us and could we go immediately to pick him up. I was lying on a sofa with my leg in plaster having a threatened miscarriage – and my husband wasn't there. I stalled for time. Could I speak to my husband and call back tomorrow? I didn't want to appear ungrateful but I really couldn't do anything immediately. I didn't want to mention the broken leg and the threatened miscarriage in case I wasn't deemed fit to be a mother. I managed to contact Wally and also telephoned a number of other people – and got conflicting advice. Quite a few thought that I should look after the baby inside me and not risk anything by going to Brazil. My gut feeling, in which I am a great believer, was that the baby in Brazil was alive and well – and ours.

The following evening we phoned back. We were told that we need not go straight away but that if we gave 'Power of Attorney' to the lawyer in Brazil, he would conduct the adoption for us and we could collect the baby when this was completed.

To all our friends and relatives, what was happening to us at this time was very exciting. To us, it was so important and nerve-racking that it was difficult to feel relaxed about the situation. The worst day for me was when I had to go to London to get the Power of Attorney document signed. In the morning I was due to go to the hospital and have the plaster on my leg removed. I had been walking around on this plaster without crutches for some time and was convinced that when it came off I would be able to walk normally. Once removed, where the plaster used to be was the hairiest leg you have ever seen, shrivelled to half its size. I looked like an emaciated gorilla. I put the leg down on the floor and it just collapsed. I couldn't stand and was back on crutches again. For the first time it all suddenly became too much. I was still pregnant and, although threatening a miscarriage, my hormones were all over the place. I somehow had to get to London that afternoon to sign the Power of Attorney. Wally was still away and I couldn't walk. I sat down in the hospital and cried – I just felt that I couldn't go on any more. It all seemed too difficult and I began to doubt if we could ever do it.

Of course I bounced back again. My friend Angie who had taken me to the hospital supplied me with tissues and drove me home. I telephoned my brother-in-law and he agreed to drive me up to London and wait for me in the car outside the lawyer's office. But first I had to shave that hairy leg!

We had a phone call from Brazil a few days later asking what we wanted to call the baby. They needed his name for the documents and we had two hours to decide. Now if you have nine months to choose a name, you take nine months. If you have only two hours, you take only two hours. After furiously writing lists and making eliminations, we came up with the names Thomas Oliver.

Towards the end of February 1985, having finally lost the baby I was carrying, we set off for Rio. We were laden with an empty carry-cot, fifty bottles of pre-sterilized SMA milk, some tiny baby clothes, and the Dr Spock book which we read all the way over on the plane. Thomas was five weeks old. We didn't know anything about babies, not having had the nine months of antenatal classes to prepare us. Wally took time off work and was able to become more involved than most fathers when their wives are in hospital breast-feeding a new baby.

We spent a night in Rio, which confirmed our view that we were doing the right thing. Seeing the streets full of abandoned children begging is a sight we will never forget. The following morning we took a plane to Florianopolis, an island off the coast of southern Brazil, to meet Thomas.

At the airport we were met by Jamir, Coletta, their family and friends, and a little brown sleeping baby with a bunch of flowers for us. We went back to Jamir's flat and spent the rest of the day learning how to change nappies, sterilize bottles and getting to know Thomas. We were staying in a hotel, so that night we were on our own. Thomas was on two-hour feeds and we spent the whole night rushing around dabbing and stabbing at both ends of him, hardly getting a wink of sleep. When he finally fell asleep he snored, and every time his breathing pattern changed we woke up.

We spent four days in Florianopolis. Jamir and his family were wonderfully hospitable, looking after us and taking us around the island. I just remember feeling very tired and not really being able to appreciate it fully. When Thomas is older we will take him back and really explore it properly. Eventually we said our goodbyes to Jamir, Coletta and family and boarded the plane back to Rio where we were staying one night on our way home.

The sterilized milk that we had brought from the UK made Thomas sick, so we were down to powdered milk and sterilizing bottles. In Florianopolis I had been lent an electric sterilizer, but in Rio I had to boil bottles in the hotel kitchen. The cooks were making a three-course dinner. I couldn't speak a word of Portuguese and waiting for those bottles to boil was the longest ten minutes of my life!

The next day we took the last leg of our journey home. We still felt very inexperienced as parents. On the plane we thought everyone must be wondering why it took two of us to change a nappy or give him a feed. Changing a nappy in an aeroplane lavatory isn't easy at the best of times, but if you don't know what you are doing it's even more difficult! I thought I was doing very well with Thomas lying on the lavatory seat when, all of a sudden, he shot this enormous poo all down the wall. I cleaned him up, shouted for Wally to take him from me and set about cleaning the wall. By this time a long queue had formed down the aisle of the plane.

We arrived back at Heathrow on the first of March having been gone exactly seven days. We had a few problems at Immigration, but eventually came through with a three-month visa for Thomas, renewable until we had formally adopted him in this country. My sister, then heavily pregnant with her second child, came to meet us and we drove back to our house in Sheen. My mother and all our neighbours were out on the street to welcome us. It was a wonderful reception.

We soon settled in at home. Thomas was a marvellous baby, happy, healthy and smiling all the time. He also ate heartily and grew at an amazing rate. By the time he was christened in May, he had grown out of three outfits that I had selected for him. In the end it was a question of what fitted him on the day. Jamir and Coletta managed to come over for his christening which we were all thrilled about.

Shortly after the christening we went on holiday to Spain. The Spanish, of course, love babies and the waitresses whisked Thomas off to the kitchen while we ate our dinner in the evening. He loved the sunshine and had his first swim. I started to feel sick while we were there. I tried to ignore it, but by the end of the first week I had developed a terrible stomach upset.

When we got home I did a home pregnancy test which proved negative, but still I carried on feeling sick. I got the chemist to do one and he got a negative result too. In the few years that I was trying to conceive I must have spent a fortune on those kits but, of course, the truth is that when you are pregnant you just know. After all, how did our grandmothers manage? Even after all the tests I did I've never managed to aim the pee straight into those little sterilized pots they give you. I always ended up with it all over my hands and then the label would get wet and my name all smudged. No wonder you sometimes get the wrong result.

Eventually I got a positive result, but I had started to bleed. I was given the usual advice of bed-rest – but of course that was out of the question as I had Thomas to look after. Personally, I don't think it makes any difference what you do. If the baby is all right it will stay; if it is not, it won't. I decided that the best thing to do was to have a scan and see what was there. I wasn't particularly worried about having another miscarriage, as I was very happy to adopt another baby from Brazil. It seemed much easier than having to get through nine months of pregnancy and then giving birth. The scan proved that I had conceived twins. One had decided to leave, but the other was growing healthily. I should have been over the moon with excitement at this news, but all I could think of was, 'Oh my God, I've actually got to go through with this now'. Perhaps part of my difficulty in having a successful pregnancy was my fear of having to go through childbirth – and as for 'natural' childbirth, I had it down on my notes from my very first hospital visit that I wanted an epidural and any other medical intervention that they had to hand.

Pregnancy was every bit as unpleasant as I had suspected it would be. I seem to remember month five being quite reasonable, but that was all. I think my body decided that it was too old for this. The term geriatric, that they use to describe older mothers, certainly felt right for me, and carrying one baby inside and another in my arms was all too much. By the end of nine months I was like a cripple and could hardly walk down the road. I was also fainting and throwing up regularly, including all over the front door of a very nice Peking restaurant that had just opened in Sheen. I believe that it is still in business, but with no thanks to me.

However, on 5 February 1986, eleven months after we had returned home with Thomas, I gave birth to Lucy, with epidural, forceps and all the other medical intervention that Queen Mary's Hospital, Roehampton could muster. Wally was in control of my right leg and I was in control of nothing.

I have to say that my feelings on being presented with Lucy were much the same as on first meeting Thomas: 'Oh, it's a baby'. I felt I had to get to know them both. The only difference was that this one was a bit messier. We still hadn't decided on a name in the delivery room. I was keen to call her Daisy and thought that Wally would give in after all that I had been through, but he said that it sounded like a milkmaid, so that was that.

I have tried to erase the next few months from my memory. My hair which had always been curly went straight and fell out. So did most of my fillings, and I felt as though I was falling to pieces. Lucy screamed until one o'clock in the morning and Thomas started teething. We have two photographs on our dining room wall, one of each of the children's christening. In Thomas's, I am romping round the garden kicking my legs in the air and generally behaving badly. In Lucy's, I've got a fat face, straight hair and a wan, watery smile. When I look back on those photos, it all comes back to me.

As I write now, they are nearly 4 and 5 years old, one fair, one dark. I love them equally and can't imagine life without them. I can still kick my legs in the air and my curls have come back!

I don't know how many people have adopted from abroad and had their own child, but I feel very lucky to have done both. Much has been written about the joys of having your own child, and I don't think I could add to that. Not so much is known about adopting from abroad. I feel that we have 'made' Thomas' life just as much as if we had conceived him ourselves. When I watch him now growing up healthily and happily, riding his bike, running into school with his friends or being a shepherd in the nativity play, I am struck by how none of this would have been possible without us – and I realize that it is the most important thing we have done in our lives.

There are critics of inter-country adoption. There are people who want to know about 'culture'. What do they mean by culture? It used to mean art galleries and opera. Now it seems to mean ethnic background and reggae music. Brazil is a beautiful country, and when the children are older we will take them to visit it. But it is extremely corrupt and has a great social divide. A rich minority, vast shanty towns, very little birth-control, huge poverty-stricken families, drink and drug problems and thousands of children living on the streets. Is that culture? I don't think so.

WALLY'S STORY

It was, of course, Susie's idea. I had always regarded myself as an unconventional person and, compared to a lifelong clerical assistant, I suppose I am. Adopting a child was unfamiliar territory to me. I should have been attracted by that fact, but felt very uncertain. At that time I knew only one couple who had done it and they had adopted in the UK. My nervousness about the whole process proved how conventional I really am. Deep down I didn't really believe that adopting would be necessary. A man of my virility, I thought, was bound to sire an heir sooner or later. Even if Susie had problems, my super potency, I believed, would overcome all obstacles and pull us through in the end. It was when the 'end' seemed to be an infinite distance away that I began to have doubts.

In the back of my mind, I knew that I didn't want to set our hopes too high. Television programmes proved inter-country adoption was possible, but they gave the impression of immense difficulty, considerable luck and a hint of illegality. Having done it, of course, I now know several people who have adopted from abroad, one of whom worked for me in a previous employment. I can recall him telling me of family problems he was having while trying to go through the adoption process. Showing sympathy wasn't covered in my management handbook, so I suspect that I turned my well-trained blind eye and deaf ear to his problems whilst telling him to pull himself together. Luckily, we were never on the receiving end of such an ignorant attitude.

If you are 'older' – i.e. over 30 or so – the conventional routes to adoption in the UK are more or less closed. The availability of contraception, the openness of unmarried or single-parent mothers, mean that comparatively few children are available for adoption – thankfully. Adopting an older child or a child with physical or mental problems was a possibility, but we couldn't bring ourselves to feel comfortable about that route. When Susie started enquiring about inter-country adoption, we discovered that the local authorities couldn't really help. It was not a case of unwillingness. Every individual that we spoke to was sympathetic, but didn't have either the time or the mechanisms to offer help.

The idea of adopting from abroad grew on me as I began to believe that it could really happen, thanks to Susie's dogged determination. Left to me it would probably never have succeeded. Once I had warmed to the idea I would have tried, but my ability to bounce back and overcome obstacles falls somewhat short of Susie's. I am eternally in her debt for the happy outcome of her determination. I can even forgive her equal determination for leaving cheque-book stubs blank and her refusal to collect receipts. It seems an eminently fair swop. Having discovered that a friend from university (whom I hadn't seen for twenty years) had adopted from abroad, the idea seemed less strange. I had a reference point and was reassured by it.

There was a fair amount of documentation needed, but nothing that struck me as being unreasonable and nothing terribly difficult to get hold of. It seemed odd to have to 'prove' that you are worthy of parenthood. After all, for the natural process all you have to be is physically capable of breeding. Of course, placing a child by choice involves some degree of certainty that the child's welfare will be secure. One of the necessary documents we had to have was a satisfactory 'home study' report. I wasn't sure what the home study test would be looking for. We were human, reasonably sane and undoubtedly middle class. We had established this latter status by Susie coming down one level and pulling me up to meet her. Alison Austin (the independent social worker who did our study) told us about the range of people for whom she had performed studies, which relaxed us. Nothing magical was sought. Our natural attitudes, warts and all, were good enough to indicate our 'suitability'.

Part of the medical documentation enquired about fertility. On reflection, I can't remember why this was necessary. My friend from university and, as I subsequently discovered, yet another colleague of mine had both added a foreign adopted child to their existing natural families. I had assumed that infertile couples were given greater priority. Perhaps not. Susie had doctors' reports galore indicating problems with conception. I was invited to donate sperm for testing and somewhat to my surprise achieved a reasonable rating on the Richter scale − or whatever is the sperm-count equivalent.

In one sense, our Brazil trip was remarkably easy. All credit was due to Jamir and Coletta for their meticulous efforts on our behalf. We arrived when Thomas was five weeks old. He was legally ours; we had adopted him by proxy in the Brazilian juvenile courts. It amused us to read that Thomas, via his lawyer, had agreed to take us on as parents. I will remind him of this obligation in later years if he starts to prove difficult! Jamir had translated all the documents into English − court proceedings, registration of birth, adoption certificate. Each was clearly labelled, stamped to show authenticity and had a reference to the appropriate part of the Brazilian judicial system. There was very little for us to do. We met the 'minors judge' out of courtesy and gratitude rather than necessity. Jamir had organized a passport for Thomas which we had to collect and authorize. We met the lawyer who had acted on our (and Thomas's) behalf.

Before we went, I was apprehensive about the attitudes we might come across in Brazil. Would there be resentment at comparatively rich Europeans exporting one of their children? Certainly all the people we met were very supportive. As we were leaving our hotel in Rio to board a taxi to the airport, the hotel porter asked, 'Is he Brazilian?' I recall feeling slightly nervous. Was he going to try to take him back? I didn't understand all that he said, but he seemed to be expressing gratitude and told us to 'give him a good chance in life'.

No one questioned the ethics or the validity of what we were doing. Certainly no one seemed concerned that Thomas was moving away from his 'birth culture' and going to live in a foreign country.

It is easy to make generalized statements warning about mixing different races and cultures. At the general level, such concern is valid and guidelines and standards are needed to prevent exploitation and abuse. However, the welfare of the child and his or her alternatives in life are surely what matter. Admittedly, we would have taken second place in the Brazilian adoption queue had a local placement been possible. It wasn't – and the welfare of Thomas was the top priority. In my view, it is better to treat each case individually than have generalized rules that benefit no one. In today's society of mixed marriages, mixed races at school and mixed religions, what does culture matter to a new-born baby? Any one of us raised in a different environment would adopt the culture of that environment. Once seen, real poverty leaves a lasting impression. Giving love and hope where it would not otherwise exist is the best gift of all. Giving protein and the wherewithal to live isn't too bad a gift either.

Once we had arrived back in the UK, Thomas took on the role of celebrity status in our little corner of East Sheen. Family, friends and neighbours were extremely supportive – and have been ever since. Thomas has developed well. He is an active and popular little boy and fits in well at the local state school. Thomas knows that he is Brazilian. He boasts about his permanent sun-tan and will no doubt grow into a handsome and popular young man. He is aware that he came from 'another lady's tummy' before mummy and daddy came to collect him. This story is so routine to him now that when he starts to tell it he often tires of it halfway through and changes the subject (except where he improves the story by involving pirates or ghostbusters). Thomas knows that Lucy came from 'mummy's tummy'. He still takes pride in saying that this may be where girls come from, but *real* boys come in big jumbo jets from Brazil.

Once ensconced back in the UK, we were 'inspected for suitability' by a young social worker. This was a prerequisite step to getting Thomas legally adopted over here. The young girl tackled her challenge with enthusiasm – and with considerable guidance from Susie. I occasionally wonder what the authorities would have done if we were deemed unsuitable, and yet we were legal adoptive parents in Brazil. Thankfully this was a challenge that proved irrelevant!

We made two visits to the Wandsworth court. On our first visit we were told that we needed a document showing the mother's consent to the adoption. We had a version of this, but apparently confirmation is needed when the child is 6 months old. This seemed rather like signing a hire purchase agreement and having a 'cooling-off period' in which you could change your mind. The judge was very kind. He assured us that this was in everyone's interest and would make the adoption absolutely watertight. It would also guarantee that Thomas would have no problems in later life. Of what kind I cannot imagine! I got the impression that, even if we were to fail in finding Thomas's natural mother and getting her signature, the legal effort of trying would be sufficient. We should have anticipated this, or rather our young social worker perhaps should have known. That's just a reflection of her inexperience – she's probably the local expert by now! This delayed the process by a few months, but allowed us to have two celebratory parties. I can see some logic in this protection mechanism, but it must be a harrowing experience for the natural mother.

Lucy's birth, for some people, confirmed a piece of folklore. Comments like, 'this often happens', 'it's because you relax' and 'I know someone who adopted and subsequently . . .' were frequently made. There may be some valid medical or psychological principle involved here, but I can remember one circular conversation with some people at a party who were relating this coincidence. The people they had 'heard about' were friends of friends – and happened to be us. Perhaps these folklore statistics are distorted after all.

People occasionally ask how I regard my two children. Do I treat them differently? How did I 'bond' to my adopted child compared to my natural one? When we went to collect Thomas I wondered how long it would take until I truly felt a father to him. Since knowing that he was ours it had taken a few weeks to adopt him legally in Brazil and to arrange our journey. We were both healthy and had read a lot of books on babies, but of course we had some concerns. How would we bond to a strange baby?

Most people see their first baby when he or she is very tiny, somewhat wrinkled and rather messy. Our first glimpse was of a peacefully sleeping, unwrinkled 6-week-old boy – looking every bit like someone else's child. Unlike with Lucy one year later – 'she's got your eyes and my dimples' – there were no obvious cross-reference points.

Our feelings of excitement were tinged with anxiety. We were far from home and, unlike the pregnant mum and anxious dad, we had not been fully class-trained as to what to expect. The natural parent always has someone to turn to. Someone can always answer the question, 'What does that sound mean?' or 'Should he be doing that?' An authoritative voice is there to reassure that all is well. With no one to refer to, other than the Doctor Spock book, we didn't have that reassurance: a noise in the middle of the night, for us, meant a complete inspection of both the baby and the reference book index. In my first few hours with Thomas, I had a level of involvement with him equivalent to several days with Lucy. It strikes me that it is involvement that creates bonding, not the process of watching a child being born.

Some fathers choose to be present at the birth, some don't. There is not a lot for the father to do — indeed there is very little that he is qualified to do unless he is part of the medical team. In theory he gives support and comfort to the mother, but his role is really that of privileged spectator.

My expectations were based on what other fathers had told me and what I had read. They were also influenced by the process I had gone through with Thomas. I expected to get instantly with Lucy the level of bonding that I had reached with Thomas. Not so. The books, the tales and the hype are probably misleading. Rather like going to see the play that has rave reviews, one can expect too much. I wouldn't have missed it for the world, but natural birth didn't produce the clean, quiet and nicely-robed little baby that I was used to. It was only when I had become as involved with Lucy as I had been with Thomas that the bonds were created. That took several days. The modern UK hospital, unlike the one-star Brazilian hotel, is equipped to handle everything for you — and does so. I wonder how many parents worry about whether they are as bonded at the moment of birth as they feel they should be. My advice to any expectant parent is to forget the hype. Forget what you believe you are supposed to feel. Be assured that there are various routes to bonding: they all hinge on involvement and they all take time. How long it takes is not important.

My experience with Thomas convinces me that there are such things as 'genetic imprints'. Where else would he have got his innate ball skills and his passion for football? Not from me. I can already see the day when playing football with Dad is no longer a challenge for him. Thomas is sufficiently kind and charming that I know he will continue longer than necessary — for my sake, not his. It may be the natural desire of every man to create a son in his image, but I can truly say that with Thomas I have beaten the system! It would be a cruel twist of fate if he were to take on my natural looks and ball skills.

Thomas has the charm that I saw in many of the Brazilian people. He also has the cunning guile. I am reminded of the begging boys in Rio. Most of these were probably no more than eight years old and operated in pairs, one asking to clean your shoes, the other surreptitiously spreading dog-dirt on them under the table. Thomas has that charming cunning.

'Is there any history of this in the family?' When doctors ask this question, as they do from time to time, it never fails to amuse us. We have used all the variations of a possible answer, so we now reply in a rather factual and boring way. Thomas has the interesting challenge of creating his own reference points in life. Whatever genetic inheritances I carry with me and whatever may eventually strike me down, he is spared. I don't know what hindrances not being able to answer such questions will bring – I suspect very few.

'Which of you does he take after?' This is another question that never fails to raise a smile. It also raises a question of concern about the enquirer's eyesight. Some people have even asked us if Thomas and Lucy are twins – a question almost guaranteeing a taxi-ride to the nearest optician. Although they look different, they are close in both age and whatever the experience of being part of the same family brings. This is the common culture that they share, and I guess it shows.

We are extremely lucky to have done what we have done and have the best of possible combinations. One boy and one girl, one dark and one fair, one adopted and one natural. Each equal to the other in every sense. Legally equal. Equal in life's opportunities. Equally loved by parents, relatives and friends. An ideal family.

5 Brazilian bounty

John and Mary Hunt

For eight years John and Mary had been hoping for a family. They met their Brazilian friends Emilio and Vittoria through a mutual acquaintance at the large research laboratory where Emilio worked. Emilio had come to Britain to work on his PhD, and the couple were almost ready to return home.

HOW IT STARTED (JOHN)

'But there are thousands of unwanted babies in Brazil!' exclaimed Emilio as we sat talking. 'When I go back, I shall make some enquiries for you.'

This was just one of the lines we were to follow up. We had, at that stage, been trying for a family for eight years, and things were reaching crisis point. Even then, we were still suffering the interminable trials of infertility tests which had led us nowhere; indeed, many had simply wasted our time. I was then 37 and Mary 33 years old. We had also investigated adoption in Britain and applied to our county Social Services Department, as well as other agencies. Our local agency had by then strung us along for three years, saying, 'we have no young children available now, but apply again in three months' time, as the position is continually changing.' In the end we had gone to them again, and they admitted that they couldn't really have considered us anyway. In our area, the rate at which children became available was so slow that, with the waiting list that they already had, we would eventually be debarred on age grounds. We are both regular churchgoers of separate denominations. It was, and still is, a severe disappointment that none of the religious agencies had been able to help for one reason or another.

We had therefore reached the conclusion that quite radical steps were needed and had begun to investigate the possibility of adopting a child from abroad. We had been on holiday to Sri Lanka a couple of years before, and witnessed several Swedish couples bringing brown babies aboard the homeward aeroplane. The arrangements had been made through a Swedish agency; we knew that there were (and are still) no similar British agencies, and that we would have to do most of the work ourselves.

During our mounting concern over the adequacy of infertility treatment, we had joined the National Association for the Childless (NAC), and this had proved of immense support to us. We were by now running the local group; as is often the case, sharing others' problems reduced the intensity of our own. Limited information was available then on inter-country adoption. I spent some time at the local library poring over clerical directories collecting addresses in likely countries of diocesan representatives who might help, and wrote off. A number of embassies in London were also contacted. Disappointingly again, few of the church organizations responded and none were hopeful. Of the embassies, the Brazilian response, while detached, was at least encouraging. At that time we had no particular country in mind; our objective was rather more basic.

It also happened that year that the NAC organized a specialist meeting on inter-country adoption. We were eager attenders. There were sessions on ethical implications, legal aspects, immigration, and so on. This gave us vital basic information, but what fascinated us most were the stories of a few couples who had adopted from abroad. One couple had brought their baby with them, and enterprisingly had compiled a list of procedures needed. Their baby was from Brazil. They gave us the address of their contact and we wrote off. At least we got an eventual reply, but it was not too encouraging, indicating that a wait would be needed. For any overseas adoption, the major documentational requirement was going to be a home study, and this would need to be set up at an early stage. With some trepidation we approached our county Social Services; we could only indicate that we wished to have a home study to be able to pursue the option of overseas adoption, possibly in Brazil. After some hesitation, but possibly because we had been on their books for three years with no likelihood of local adoption, they agreed. As the procedure is fairly lengthy (especially as they felt the application should go through the County Adoptions Panel in the usual way) they also agreed to begin the necessary visitations quite quickly.

Things seemed to be coming slowly into focus. Without getting too excited, and as Mary's school holidays were fast approaching, we decided to book a package holiday to Brazil. The main objective would be to have a much-needed break, but also to see something of the country and its people. We would also take the opportunity to visit both Emilio and our more recent contact, and we wrote off to them.

Before the time came for us to leave for Brazil, we had had two visits from our social worker, and were relieved that the home study process was in train. We also made enquiries of the Brazilian Consulate in London, and of several couples who had adopted in Brazil. It was hard not to get too elated, as we did not wish to be disappointed after so many other avenues had been foreclosed.

AFTER TAKE-OFF (JOHN)

The flight to Brazil was overnight from Gatwick with a stop at Recife in Brazil. We arrived at Rio de Janeiro at 6 a.m., having had little sleep, and it was a relief to be met by a tour guide and taken to our hotel. The coach passed through the awakening city centre with its modern, high-rise buildings, but in the distance we were made aware of the 'favalas' or hillside shanty towns inhabited by the poor.

Our package included two days in Rio followed by a tour spending several days at each of a number of Brazilian cities of interest, ending with a further stay in Rio. Our first stop after Rio was to be Emilio's home town, and after an enjoyable couple of days in Rio taking in as much of the ambience as we could, we caught the midday flight there. It was late afternoon when we arrived, after covering about the same distance as from London to Istanbul but remaining in the same country. I rang Emilio from the airport, and he later collected us from our hotel and took us to his home.

We had a pleasant evening chatting and sampling an exotic Brazilian fruit salad. It was good to see Emilio, Vittoria and their by now 3-year-old daughter again. Emilio explained that he had arranged for us to see the judge who was in charge of the Minors' Court the following day. This court system is the medium for adoptions in Brazil, and we could learn more of the necessary procedures.

This was a surprise, and we cancelled our pre-arranged trip to the jungle for the next day. We went with Emilio to the Minors' Court with some trepidation. It was an open, airy building with a crowd of none-too-affluent Brazilians hanging about, apparently aimlessly. We were led to a side office labelled 'Gabineti do Juiz', and sat on a settee inside. The judge had several people to see, but surprisingly soon it came to our turn. Emilio introduced us as his friends from England and, interpreting for us, explained that we had come over to learn about adoption in Brazil. The judge clearly looked upon us kindly, and told us that adoption for us would be possible, provided both of us were at least 30 years old and had been married for five years. Rather different priorities than at home! I asked through Emilio what documents would be needed. Copies of our passports was the first reply, but there were other requirements that could be discussed later. We asked how we ought to go about finding a child, and the judge suggested we ask at the maternity hospital. But – and here came the bolt from the blue – he said he did have a baby registered. Looking at Mary, he said, 'with blue eyes like yours'. If we wished to see the baby, we would be welcome. Of course we jumped at the chance, not without a mixture of nervousness and disbelief that things at last were really happening, suddenly almost too fast to put any brakes on.

The judge called for 'the psychologist', Doctora Julia, and introduced us. She would take us to see the baby and his mother. We set off in Emilio's car along the dusty Brazilian streets. Julia told us that the baby was a little boy. The mother was unmarried, almost destitute and was not able to care for a baby as well as hold down a job. Eventually, Julia enquired at one house as to where the mother and baby might be: it seemed the mother was staying anywhere she could for a few days at a time. As we waited, I remember wondering whether this experience would be 'it', and felt a growing sense of apprehension; this was a completely new situation, one that we could not politely back away from, even assuming we wanted to; all we could do then was to wait and see. After some minutes Julia returned and we drove out of town to a new estate of simple single-storey houses with corrugated roofs. Julia went in first, then we were beckoned inside. The house was simply furnished and spotlessly clean. We were invited to sit down on a low settee in the main room. Several girls appeared and went away – it was not clear which, if any, was the mother of the baby. And then the baby was produced. Like all small babies to strangers, he somehow lacked individuality; he was fast asleep, clothed only in a thin muslin nappy in the Brazilian heat. Mary indicated for me to hold him first. It would be dishonest and unrealistic to expect that an instantaneous relationship would be experienced. I remember thinking 'was this to be my son?' I held him for quite some time, until a wet presence began to make itself known. One of the Brazilian girls dutifully took him away and brought him back with another nappy. Mary held him for a little while, and we both realized that this was the chance for which we had waited so long. Julia, who had disappeared to another room, came back presently. On hearing our decision, she tried to telephone the court several times but failed to get through. A short, curly-haired girl appeared: she was introduced to us as the baby's mother, Rosita. It became clear that Julia had been talking to her while we had been holding the baby. We exchanged some pleasantries via Emilio. Julia suggested that we go back to the court, as the judge finished his business at midday. We took some photographs of everyone outside the house, then all climbed into Emilio's car.

Back at the court, the judge was pleased with our decision and anxious to make us guardians right away. This would not give us the right to take the baby out of the country (we would have to adopt him in Brazil first), but would transfer the baby to our care. A form was produced, and the judge asked if we could decide on the name for the baby right away as it would simplify the procedures; the mother had not yet registered the birth, although she had called him 'Rodrigo'.

After everything that had happened, to make such a decision in half a minute was not easy. Moreover, Brazilians normally have three forenames. We decided to keep 'Rodrigo' for his middle name, and after some further deliberation chose 'William' and 'Benjamin' as his other Christian names. The form was duly signed. Rosita's hand was understandably very shaky. The judge disappeared for his lunch. This left us wondering what to do with William. Here we were, in a strange place, due to leave the next day, without the possibility of taking him with us. I asked Julia if there was an orphanage where we could pay to have him looked after. She explained that such facilities are not common in Brazil: it is more usual to rely on one's own family, friends and neighbours. Eventually, she said she thought she knew of a lady called Lucia who might help, and telephoned her. Almost incredibly, she agreed, and further, to take on the job that afternoon! This was Brazilian bounty indeed. Rosita gave us a carrier bag with a few simple items she had for William. It included a small parcel wrapped up tightly in elastoplast which she asked Mary to look after very carefully. It contained the umbilicus which, as in other cultures, is kept to place under the child's pillow during illness or planted under a tree for good luck.

After a lunch with everyone – including Rosita – at a fish restaurant, we set about further arrangements. Mary and Julia took William to Lucia's house. I went with Emilio and Rosita to the Registry of Births, which looked from the outside like a Mexican bar. William's certificate was typed out before us on a pre-war typewriter. We then took Rosita back to the family she was staying with and joined the others at Lucia's house.

Lucia and her neighbours had rallied round, and there was a stream of visitors bringing all manner of baby items. Nevertheless, Mary went out on a shopping spree, and I had my first experience of buying disposable nappies. Julia had made a doctor's appointment and we went off in Emilio's car again, which was by now overheating rather badly. After a long wait at the doctor's practice, William was examined and thankfully pronounced fit and healthy. I remembered that a medical report is one of the requirements in the UK, and got the doctor to write one out, which he did on a scrap of paper in indecipherable Portuguese.

Emilio's car was giving severe problems with all the running around, so he went directly home. Julia's boyfriend was summoned and he took us back to Lucia's house where we settled William down for the night. In our absence, more goodies had been delivered by well-wishers, including a cot. Eventually Mary and I managed to get away and we were taken back to our hotel where, tired, overwhelmed, both of us with headaches but nevertheless overjoyed, we went to bed.

THE NEXT STEPS (JOHN)

Our tour was due to leave the city the next afternoon. One of the options was to break off and spend longer here, then return to England. However, this would not have served a useful purpose, as the judge had told us he could get the preliminary documentation completed the following morning. So we decided to continue with the tour, and having got up bright and early we left our luggage for the others on the tour to bring to the airport. We then drew out further supplies of cruzeiros from the hotel cashier to buy more baby items later and made our way by taxi to the Minors' Court once more.

We were met by Rosita and went to the judge's office. Emilio also arrived – he had managed to get his car fixed. We were ushered into a clerk's room where he drafted a document which would enable adoption proceedings to start. Mary, in a mixture of languages, got talking to Rosita. Photographs and postcards were exchanged. Rosita was worried about the non-appearance of 'Rodrigo', but was reassured that he was being looked after. She told Mary she was a Catholic (so is Mary: thus a common factor emerged) and that she could play the piano and would like 'Rodrigo' to learn. I spent some time looking through the file of a US couple who had adopted there, noting down with Emilio's help the types of document required. Eventually, we were told the judge had approved the clerk's draft and when it had been typed out we went to sign in front of him. I was concerned that we did not yet have a mother's consent, which I knew to be vital for British entry clearance procedures to begin. Not being prepared on this trip, we did not have the necessary form of words, and I hastily drafted out what I could remember. Julia translated it into Portuguese, saying that a similar document would be needed for Brazil too. The clerk typed it up, and Rosita signed. I thought that signing before the judge would count, but he said that it should be notarized. By then, the court's paperwork was complete, so we left and went downtown, dropping off Mary and Julia to do more baby shopping. Emilio, Rosita and I went to the Notary's office, but – the first blow – it was closed for the long lunch break and there was no time before our plane left. Still, I thought, perhaps with the court stamp on it it might be acceptable at home. How wrong this turned out to be – but not for that reason. Emilio and I dropped Rosita off at the bus station and exchanged farewell hugs. We went to Lucia's house, arriving before Mary and Julia, and saw William again, fast asleep. How sweet he was! We would soon have to leave him in Lucia's care for several months at least. I sorted out financial arrangements with Lucia, who was going to hire another maid. Mary and Julia returned, loaded to the gunwales with a baby bath, saucepans, bottles and other unfamiliar trappings of parenthood. It was then time to go, and tearfully bidding expressions of deep gratitude we bundled into Emilio's car again and headed for the airport. Our fellow travellers were astounded at what we had achieved in the space of thirty-six hours.

We had a lovely time on the rest of our Brazilian holiday. We phoned Julia nearly every day to learn how William was. In one other city we met the other contact we had obtained in England. She was very pleased to hear that we had 'scored' already, because she would have been unable to help us right away. Back in Rio before we left for England, we had a few days' stability and set about getting papers translated. At this stage we were unsure of precisely what would be needed at home. We went to the British Consulate and had an interview with one of the vice-consuls. She began by insisting that we could not take William back to England straight away. When we explained that we could not do this in any case she calmed down. She was unsure of the details of the procedure for entry clearance for adoptees, but agreed to set it in train by telexing the Home Office. We paid the fee for this, as well as for the response.

BACK HOME, EPISODE ONE (JOHN)

Once back in England we began an anxious time in getting documents together to satisfy two not exactly compatible systems: first, the documentation for Brazil, secondly the procedures for William's entry clearance, which we had decided to pursue. This last decision was not taken lightly. Many couples bring their overseas-adopted babies into Britain without entry clearance. We felt we should do things properly, and being a civil servant (albeit a scientist) I felt better than averagely-placed to tackle the bureaucracy.

With regard to the Brazilian requirements we visited our Social Services Department, who were pleased for us but could not help displaying signs of being slightly 'miffed' that for once the customers were in the driving seat. We had more visits to set up the home study. They still felt the case should go to the County Adoptions Panel, which met once a month. The best that could be done would be to aim for the one in two months' time. Agreement had to be obtained from the Panel for the normally confidential home study to be taken by us to a third party; fortunately this was forthcoming. We also set about getting medicals, statements from our doctor, bank manager, employers, etc., all of which had to be signed before a Notary Public. Certified copies of passports, birth and marriage certificates were needed. With all these arrangements, things became rather fraught.

One afternoon, Mary came home late and in tears. She had lost the notarized certificate from the bank manager which she had picked up during her school lunch-hour. She had even been through the school rubbish bin to try and find it. We sat down over a cup of tea and went through the possibilities. The only place she had been unable to check was an office she had visited during the lunch-hour but which was now closed. Next morning she telephoned; the form had been found in its envelope and kept for her.

Soon we had all the forms bar one – the home study. Only when the Adoption Panel had approved our application could we obtain it. In parallel with this, we had to set up William's British entry clearance. I got through to the right department at the Home Office and had a file prepared. They had received a telex from Rio but were not happy with how the matter had been initiated. They sent us very detailed forms asking questions about us, William and his parentage. They asked for the medical we had had the foresight to have carried out and trans-lated. Then the big blow – Rosita's declaration was not acceptable. This was because it had been signed when William was only 3 weeks old. British law demands that the declaration is signed after six weeks. I endeavoured to get a copy of the right form locally. The Social Services Department and County Court both said the other should have a copy. Eventually one was obtained by photocopying a copy of the appro-priate Government White Paper. We now had the problem of getting the form to Brazil to be signed by Rosita and returned. I posted one copy to Julia and one to the local British consular representative before whom the form was best signed.

Meanwhile, I investigated all sorts of ways of getting the precious form back. One cannot trust the post in Brazil. A little parcel we had sent within Brazil, even when registered, had already gone missing. I contacted various carrier agencies, none of whom would accept payment in Britain for a return delivery. Furthermore, on speaking to Julia by telephone on one of our regular 'how's William?' calls (thank heaven for direct dialling, even at £1 a minute) she said she would not trust the couriers, judging by the state of their offices.

The difficulty of getting the form back became secondary, however, because we soon had another setback. Julia had received the form. It was some days before she was able to track Rosita down and arrange an appointment with the local British consular representative. However, on arriving at his office, they found he had gone to the airport to meet someone. Rosita had got upset and was now refusing to sign anything. When the news of this reached Mary she was devastated; I was away on duty in the North at the time, and she told me the news when I rang from a call box at one of the motorway service areas on the M6. I rang back later from my hotel and tried to see how we could pick up the pieces. Julia had said that she would try again, but Mary was worried because of Rosita's attitude. However, we heard a few days later that Rosita had calmed down, and then that the precious form had been signed. Now came the problem of getting it back. Julia would trust only personal contact. We were in the process of sorting out a courier when Julia told us she had heard of someone coming to England from Emilio's institute. After making contact with the people at this end, I found out that he would be having a meeting soon after his arrival with someone from my laboratory! A couple of weeks later, the form arrived on our doormat. It was hastily sent by recorded delivery to the Home Office to complete the application for entry clearance.

Two months had now passed since we had returned to England. Mary in particular was getting anxious that we would lose credibility. We therefore decided that as soon as our documents for Brazil were ready, Mary would take them over, put the process in hand, and be with William. I would stay at my job until the British entry clearance was complete. We had been very fortunate in that the airline, in selling us excursion tickets, had agreed to concede a change of return date in view of what we were doing and the uncertainty surrounding completion. All we needed now was for the Adoption Panel to clear us so that we could get our home study. On the day of the hearing I was delayed at a meeting in London, but got back home to find Mary in a state again: the Panel had approved our application, but only on condition that our medicals were in order. They had not arrived from our GP, whom we had had to pay privately to do them.

We were, of course, furious. The Panel would have been within their rights to reject our application. We bombarded our surgery with telephone calls and a visit to the practice supervisor. However, it was not for another two days that we heard from our social worker that our GP had telephoned her to confirm there were no problems over our medicals, and no apology had been forthcoming. However, our social worker was now able to complete the home study.

Mary booked her flight for ten days hence. This was tight, but it gave us just enough time for the home study to be finished and notarized, taken to London with all our other documents to be stamped at the Brazilian Consulate, then collected on the day of Mary's departure. It felt rather like a chapter from a le Carré novel, as I left Mary on a bench in Hyde Park while I got the set of documents back from the Consulate and handed them over. We then caught the Piccadilly Line to Heathrow. I stayed with Mary for a little while, then had to leave before the time came for her to check in so as to be able to get back home the same night.

BACK TO BRAZIL (MARY)

There was a three-to-four hour wait before my flight would be called so I settled down in a quiet place surrounded by luggage, including a new baby buggy. My feelings were mixed. I couldn't wait to see William again, yet I was apprehensive about the flight and the unknown time I would have to be on my own in Brazil. I took out my rosary and was deep in thought when my college friend arrived unexpectedly to see me off. We talked endlessly and had a bite to eat before my flight was called. The plane was delayed by two hours, and once underway the trip was long (twelve hours) but uneventful. In Rio I was relieved to hear the announcement that all connecting flights within Brazil had been held back. I claimed my luggage, found my way round to the internal flight lounge and was soon on the last leg of the journey to be reunited with William. Just before landing I changed into a T-shirt and skirt because I knew the tropical sun would be beating down fiercely, as by now it was midday.

Once the airport formalities were over I was delighted to see three smiling faces pressed up against the glass door, waving and gesticulating to me. Now the smattering of Portuguese I had been teaching myself with the aid of tapes and so on was to be put to the test, for Lucia and her family spoke very little English.

'Onde William?' I enquired.

'Em casa', was the reply.

'Tudo bem?' I continued.

'Oh sim'.

The heat in the well-ventilated car was almost unbearable, and it felt so good to be in an air-conditioned room in the house. William was snuggled in a swinging hammock in a bedroom. He was by then a very big and chubby baby, 3 months old, clothed only in a muslin nappy. I spoke gently to him. He opened his eyes and gave me a huge smile. I let him play with my fingers for a while and kissed him. I felt so happy. I had decided to take one photo a day until John joined us. We had not been able to join in parentcraft classes in England, but I had equipped myself with a baby book and common sense and was very grateful to Lucia, who painstakingly took me through William's full daily routine, preparing and administering bottle feeds, nappy-changing, tepid bathing and the very early morning walk in the sunshine for five minutes for him to develop his daily dose of vitamin D. Vitamins B and C were given by drops. He had thrived under Lucia's loving care and I knew we had been right to trust her. Now he had five females looking after him, so his every whimper was attended to with infinite solicitude.

One of my first tasks was to have the papers translated into Portuguese by a translator recommended by the court. After the weekend was over I met Julia again and she took me to the translator, who could do the job in a week. All the papers were then lodged at the court. I was called there on several occasions with William to see the judge and social workers. The judge also allowed Rosita to make further contact at the court to get to know me better. The court visits were rather nerve-racking times, for although I could follow the gist of the proceedings, often I would do little more than sit calmly cradling William in my arms and smile and nod appropriately. I had by this time gained a wide vocabulary for child-care needs and everyday living around the house, but this was not entirely appropriate here!

John was in constant touch by letter and telephone, sharing the ups and downs of officialdom with me and hoping to join me before too long. I was able to sample and collect souvenirs of local life both for myself and for William to treasure. I went with Lucia to the fish and produce market at 6 a.m. to feast my eyes on the tropical fare and help purchase a week's supply. Several youngsters were hired to carry huge water-melons, whole hands of bananas, eggs, fish, etc. to the car. The supermarkets and department stores were similar to those at home. Lucia's house was spotless, cleaned throughout every day, and all laundry was hand-washed in cold water. I did, however, have to get

used to local wildlife – huge ants, cockroaches and venomous cater-
pillars, but luckily no tarantulas. The television was a good source of
entertainment. The Brazilians are avid soap opera watchers. I also
joined in with a samba school. Lucia's friends, neighbours and
relatives were always popping in to say 'Bom dia' and to cuddle
William. The 'hands on' is very much the Brazilian way with babies.
They were all very supportive of what we were doing and helped to
keep my spirits up during the wait.

BACK HOME, EPISODE TWO (JOHN)

Meanwhile, back in England, I had a little breathing space, but as time
ticked by things began to get fraught again. The objective was to get
William's entry clearance. I made almost daily telephone calls to the
Home Office, the DHSS and our County Hall. A week after Mary had
left I managed to get the DHSS to extract our file and write to County
Hall for the home study. It took a week to arrive. However, they had
omitted to send a report on police checks, which they had been asked
for and which had been done for the Adoption Panel. Again I phoned
County Hall, and they agreed to send the report. Four days later it had
still not reached the DHSS. County Hall were bombarded with more
calls; a clerk looked on our file and could not find any record of its
being sent, and it would need to be retyped. So this was what we paid
rates for! It was desperately frustrating. Later that day I learnt that
the letter of which County Hall seemed to have no record had arrived;
it had been posted first class but had taken four days to get to
London.

The officials were becoming responsive to persistence now. Only the
next day I was actually telephoned by the DHSS to say our file was
being sent back to the Home Office with their recommendations. It
took three more days for it to arrive as they are sent by second-class
post, but on the day they received it they called me back to say they
were about to telex the British Consulate in Rio to allow William a
letter of consent. This was great news. My wait in England was over. I
immediately telephoned our travel firm and was booked on the plane
leaving in three days' time. It had taken three weeks since Mary
had left.

REUNION AND MURPHY (JOHN)

The trip out seemed never-ending. After the overnight flight – on
which it was difficult to sleep – there was a two-hour wait for the

connection at Rio, and another four hours' flight after that. I arrived bleary-eyed in the heat. Whilst waiting for my luggage I spotted Mary holding William outside the heavy glass airport window. I ran up and blew kisses at them. William was fast asleep, a chubby chap now of 4 months, with a creditable sun-tan. Lucia was there too, and after clearing customs she took us back to her place where I was to stay.

Julia was there briefly: she told us that the Brazilian adoption papers would soon be ready for signing and that we should be ready to go in about a week. Meanwhile we were to await her call from the court. This news was reassuring – too reassuring as it turned out, but it meant we could relax for a little while. However, it was the beginning of December, and we were hoping to be home before Christmas; with the extra travelling population things could be tricky on the airlines. For the next couple of days I learnt all about William's routine: nappy-changing, feeding, being woken up in the middle of the night, etc. Apart from Lucia and her two daughters, aged 11 and 8, she had two au pairs, and William was used to a lot of female attention. We were able to leave William in someone else's care and look around the town. I also met many of Lucia's friends and neighbours. We met Emilio and his family again and they took us on a trip. We also went out for a day with Lucia's daughters.

A week went by and we had not heard from Julia. Mary phoned her – Julia thought the papers would be ready that day, and would ring. No call. Mary telephoned again that afternoon; Julia thought that the papers would be ready the next day, but we should wait for her call. The next day was Friday, which had the frustration of the weekend coming up. We heard nothing. We at last got through to Julia at home in the late afternoon. She had not been into work due to domestic complications and was unsure how far the judge had got. We were advised to go to the court ourselves on Monday. The delay was disappointing, but we determined to make the best of things, so we went out to a restaurant with Lucia and her daughters. However, that night I woke with the most awful attack of Montezuma's revenge. I confined myself to the bedroom and bathroom (alternately) for most of Saturday, while Mary and the girls (who had not eaten the crab) enjoyed themselves shopping.

By the Monday I had recovered, but Mary had picked up an ear infection and went off to the clinic at 8 a.m. At 8.10, Julia rang saying to come to the court and to bring William, as Rosita was there. We got there by taxi at about 9 a.m. Rosita was waiting in the lobby, and ran up and hugged us all. We sat in the judge's offices for some time, chatting and exchanging presents; Rosita was keen to obtain the judge's approval. Julia then took us to the clerk's office where furious typing was going on. We signed a document. We were told we would then have to go to a notary in the town. We said '*au revoir*' to Rosita and bundled into a taxi. At this stage we were not quite sure of the objective, but Julia explained it was so that we could get William's birth certificate transferred into our names. At the Notary's office Julia somehow managed to get us to the front of the queue. The Notary looked at the documents and apparently said he would need the original birth certificate. Julia said it was at the court and needed for their purposes. After some discussion it appeared that the only solution was to get another certificate, so off we went to the registrar of births. By then it was nearly lunchtime, but Julia managed to get us let in. At first the lady in charge said we would have to wait until 3 p.m. After some bargaining and paying what seemed like a premium price, she typed out a new certificate from her ledgers. We then went back to Lucia's for lunch; Julia had to get back to the court.

This was beginning to seem like hard work in the Brazilian heat, but it turned out that we had only just started! At 2 p.m. we were back at the Notary's office, facing a large queue again. Mary did very well with her Portuguese. At first it seemed the Notary wanted until 4 p.m. the next day to produce his document. Mary managed to get him to produce it by 9 a.m. He would also need a representative of the court to sign. We telephoned Julia later to arrange this. Not a great deal more would be done that day. Things were rather frustrating – there was still a lot to do. It didn't seem as if we would get home for Christmas. One bright note was that on phoning the British Consulate in Rio I was told that William's letter of consent could be dealt with in one day.

The next day Mary and I arrived at the Notary's office. Julia and a lady from the court also arrived. We signed a handwritten entry in copperplate Portuguese in a ledger. A copy was laboriously typed out, and sewn into a folder. This was our *Escritura* which was our application to have the birth certificate changed. There was some confusion about whether to take this straight to the birth registry. We did, but the lady in charge wanted another document, the *Mandado* from the court. Into a taxi again. Progress seemed so tortuous. At the court, Julia found the *Mandado* and gave it to us; when we got back to the registry it was (typically) closed for lunch. However, we made sure that the lady had all the documents. She said she could do the birth certificate by 3.30 p.m. I asked for three copies – one can't be too careful.

The next step would be getting William's passport, so we found out

what would be needed. There seemed a formidable array of requirements; the birth certificate was only one. We would have to get new
photographs of William – some which Mary had had done already
were not the right size. We would also have to pay the fee into a bank,
for which we needed copies of a certain form. By the end of the day,
we had got the photographs done and purchased some forms from a
stationer. We also got our birth certificates after again paying what
seemed a large amount, even judging by Brazilian inflation rates
applied to the previous day's cost!

The next morning, bright and early, we went to the court with a new
birth certificate. We couldn't find Julia, but the clerk took it and put
it on our file, giving us in return a letter signed by the judge enabling
us to apply for William's passport. There was also a fee to pay. We
then found Julia, who was tied up with another case, but she directed
us to a bank where we were supposed to pay William's passport fee.
We found the bank, but the assistant at first professed to know
nothing about any way of paying a passport fee. Mary coped marvel-
lously, persisting in Portuguese, and the assistant was won over and
slowly sorted out the details, even phoning the passport office to find
out the amount of the fee.

Armed with a stamped deposit receipt and our other documents, we
took a taxi to the passport office. This, being run by the Federal
Police, was a distinctly military-style, single-storey building with bars
on the windows. We filled in all the forms and handed them over. The
official waiting time for a passport was 18 hours. This meant that if
we could get the passport the next morning, Thursday, we could leave
that afternoon. Otherwise we would have to wait until the following
Monday for the next connecting flight, the availability of which was
not certain with the Christmas rush. However, the officer realized this
was an unusual case and called his boss over. Mary overheard the boss
suggest that the mother (Rosita) might contest our right to take
William away. He would need to send one of his men to the court to
check the papers. We pointed out the judge's letter, but it cut no ice.
We left, somewhat resigned to taking the later plane.

Back at Lucia's we telephoned Julia, who was indignant. A little
while later she called back to say that the judge had spoken personally
with the Chief of Police to complain that one of the police staff had
had the temerity to mistrust his letter. We were still unsure whether
that would get us our passport early the next day, but decided to get
ready. I took a taxi downtown to the airline office, explaining to the
manager the arrangement about changing the dates of our tickets. He
would need to telex London. However, because of the time difference

the London office would be closed, so we could not finalize things anyway until the next day.

It was then lunchtime. Not bad for a morning's work, but there was still uncertainty. I fed William his lunch and he was promptly sick all over me.

That afternoon we began to make preparations to return home, telling all our new friends what was happening. Mary went to buy presents. We also received piles of presents and letters for us to deliver to people in England. So bad was the Brazilian postal service that any opportunity was taken of someone going in person.

Early on Thursday we dressed William and got to the Federal Police building before it opened at 8 a.m. The passport boss arrived late and seemed as obstinate as ever, expressing surprise that we had come so early, and saying he would still need to check Rosita's declaration. He allowed us to telephone the court, and Julia spoke to him. After some discussion he relented, and said we could have a passport in half an hour! William's little fingerprints were taken and a typewriter got into action. I took a taxi downtown straight away and went to the airline office. I just caught the supervisor, who was going out somewhere. He instructed an assistant to change our tickets for a flight of our choice. I kept my fingers crossed. Yes, the flight to Rio that day was still available, as was the connection on the Saturday night for London. Our tickets were changed and I bought William's one-way baby ticket. Near-certainty at last!

Back at Lucia's, things were in a chaotic state. We had about one hour before it was time to go. A taxi was ordered. I had done most of my packing the night before, but Mary, who had been there longer, had articles all over the house. One of the au pair girls busied herself emptying drawers directly into Mary's suitcases. I could not bear to watch. Various neighbours kept appearing, saying goodbye and giving us more presents to squash into our bulging luggage as well as all the acquired baby belongings, not to mention the stocks of boiled water, nappies, baby food, sterile bottles, etc. Lucia, who had become quite attached to William in the four months he had been in her care, could not bear to see us go; she had already said a provisional goodbye early that morning before going off to work. She spoke to us in tears from her office. Julia arrived and we thanked her for what she had done. Suddenly the taxi arrived, not the usual Volkswagen 'beetle' but a larger one which would hold all our luggage. This was piled aboard and we were whisked away.

We had left word with Rosita who had said she wanted to say goodbye to us at the airport. We waited, and sure enough a car arrived with

Rosita and an employee from the court. We had a goodbye drink, took some photographs and had a chat. Mary had come to understand Rosita over the weeks and felt it was important for her to say a final goodbye. She calmly held William in her arms for the last time as we went up to the barrier, then handed him over. For us it was an emotional moment. It must have been for her too, but she handled it well.

On the flight to Rio we at last began to unwind, but were well aware that there were still hurdles to cross. In Rio we booked into a hotel within walking distance of the British Consulate. Our connecting flight for London was in two days' time, on the Saturday.

On Friday morning I went along to the Consulate with William's passport to claim our 'letter of consent'. They made some inane queries like, had I filled in the form, and they would need to ensure I had paid the fee. I was asked to call back later in the day as the appropriate official was out, but they assured me our letter would be available. Back at the hotel we busied ourselves with sorting out the unsorted luggage. William was quite happy sitting in his buggy watching television. It struck me that we ought to confirm our flight to London, so I rang the airline. It was a good thing I did, because they could find no booking, and the flight was nearly full. I read out the flight number on the tickets – it was a plane to Paris! The fault was rectified; by now we were used to nasty moments like this. In the afternoon I went back to the Consulate, and was eventually presented with a cheap-looking piece of paper. This purported to be the vital document to get William into Britain which we had battled over for three months before returning to Brazil. I was about to go when I noticed it was a copy, and queried whether it should not be the original. The official was apologetic and rummaged in his file, eventually locating the top copy. It looked just as uninspiring, quite a contrast from the flamboyant documents produced by the Brazilians that we had grown used to.

The next day we relaxed, did some last-minute shopping and squeezed in a little sightseeing, then checked in at the airport for our flight home. Predictably, it was delayed. We met a couple from the USA who had adopted two babies in Brazil. They had had no problems with their immigration, having been given permission to bring back up to two unnamed children, thereby cutting out much of the red tape and the need to make two visits to Brazil. Nevertheless, we had nearly made it now, and again tried to relax during the flight.

DULCE DOMUM (JOHN)

We arrived at Heathrow on the Sunday afternoon. It was a cold and wet December day. William sat snugly in his buggy as we trundled him through the endless corridors towards immigration. Mary remembered we had no winter baby vests. When we arrived, there was an enormous queue for the 'foreign passports' section. We decided to try the 'British passports' queue instead. This moved very quickly. When we got to the desk with William, the officer was hesitant – he had to consult his boss. We let some people past to avoid being unpopular. There was some question of a medical for William, which we had been warned about. We pointed out what a bonny baby he was and offered to produce some medical reports. The officer returned and we were given 180 days provisional entry. We had made it at last! Quickly we claimed our luggage and passed through customs to where Mary's family and some friends were waiting to welcome us. It was nine days before Christmas. This was to be the best Christmas yet.

However, this was not the end of the story. There were still uncertainties and frustrations to go through for another fifteen months in connection with William's British adoption. Many of the procedures we had already been through were repeated, and it seemed *ad nauseam*. We were getting to be old hands. But we finally came to the end of the road when we took William to our County Court and the judge signed the adoption order. From that moment William was British, and, of course, our son for the purposes of British officialdom. For us, however, he had become our son eighteen months before in that simple house in the Brazilian heat – by the remotest chance of our being there at the right time. Some would say this could not have been planned – or could it?

6 Favourite bedtime stories

Barbara Mostyn

Barbara Mostyn differs from the other contributors in having managed to adopt two children from abroad as a single parent. This has never been against the law in Britain, yet one might infer from most of the other stories that without a partner's support the obstacle course of inter-country adoption must be even harder to overcome.

MAMA   On 15 September 1983, a beautiful baby boy was born in Delhi.

JOSHUA   At the Jeedim Hospital.

MAMA   Yes, and the doctor immediately called Mama and said, 'Your lovely baby boy is here, come as quickly as you can and adopt him'.

JOSHUA   That was me – Joshua.

MAMA   Mama flew out on Air India as fast as she could, went right to Jeedim Hospital and picked up the lovely Joshua and gave him lots of kisses.

JOSHUA   And you brought 'Gee-Gee' [the favourite stuffed toy, a small white seal].

MAMA   We took a walk in the hospital garden and saw the ladies gardening. . .

JOSHUA   And we saw some chipmunks running up the trees.

MAMA   Yes, and a few days later we took a taxi to the airport early in the morning and got on the aeroplane to fly back to London.

JOSHUA   And I had my own little bed on the aeroplane and you gave me lots of babas [bottles].

MAMA   Yes, and when we landed at Heathrow, Renee picked us up in her car and took us to Highgate and home to your own little bed.

JOSHUA   And I had a bathy and you rocked me in this chair and 'BooBoo' was there too [a special extra-large stuffed polar bear]. . . . And lots of people came to see me. (He then recites an enormous list of all the people he knows, or knew in the past.)

Ever since Joshua was 18 months old, this story has been part of our bedtime repertoire. As time goes on more detail is added about the plane journey, people we saw in Delhi, the adoption process, and what he did when he first got home. Unlike other bedtime stories, which either he tells or I read, he likes to participate in the telling of this one because we both know that it is very special – it marks the beginning of our life together.

Now at 6 years old, Joshua doesn't fully comprehend the meaning of adoption but he has positive feelings about it. The other day he informed me that he wasn't going to have children when he was an adult, he was going to adopt instead – 'because it's special'.

It was a trip to Boston that became the turning-point in our coming together. My foster daugher Lizzie and I were there in 1982, having done a house exchange for August. We spent a day with some old friends who have three lovely children, as well as very busy careers. Jean was saying how wonderful it was for women to have both a career and children these days and described a special friend in Delhi, an administrator for the Ford Foundation, who had been able to adopt two little girls through a doctor sympathetic to single women adopters. 'You're in the same situation, why don't you write to her?' she asked. I'd been telling her how I'd hoped to foster another girl as company for Lizzie, now 12 years old, when I'd been caught in a 'time warp' due to the changing fashions in British adoption policy. Lizzie is of mixed race, and in 1980 her placement with a white mother had been considered a good thing. By 1982 it was considered a bad thing – colour-coding had replaced character-matching. No, they said, I couldn't foster another mixed-race child, let alone black, and the white children were well catered for by couples and I was single. Only one social worker I talked to was interested in me when he learned that I am partially American Indian, until his colleagues informed him that the American Indian is a totally different type of Indian to the Asians!

As we enter the 1990s this 'colour-coding' fashion is finally beginning to break down, having wreaked havoc on any number of babies and children needing homes. However, at the time I wasn't prepared to fight the system. I thought a long time (six months) about adopting from India and Lizzie and I had long talks about the implications. Her main concerns were whether we would have to switch to curries as our mainstay, as she is an avid Chinese food fan as well as enjoying a wide range of other foods from French, Italian and German to Jamaican. I assured her we would continue with our usual menus which included an occasional curry. Then there were the pets – the cat, two dogs, tropical fish and gerbils. Would they be safe? I assured her they would be protected and also that they were all hers to share with another child only if she wished.

Eight months after the conversation in Boston, I wrote off to Marilyn in Delhi, who surprised me by writing back immediately and with great enthusiasm about helping another single woman to adopt. However, her personal contact – an obstetrician – obviously had babies *only*. That took some thinking about. Lizzie was now 13 years old and in school full-time, I worked full-time as well, although mostly from home; however, I had to travel fairly frequently. What would our life be like with a baby? A *baby*! Just the thought of caring for, holding, and bringing up my own adopted baby made me realize that I was being offered a wonderful opportunity, and that I had never totally come to terms with the thought that I would *never* hold my baby in my arms, never touch, smell, soothe, encourage, teach and nurture and share my life with a child throughout his or her development. Here I was in my forties, and the thought of bringing up a baby from the beginning was just thrilling!

But it took some thinking about too; was this in the best interests of the child? After all, a young child of 4 or 5 years old with memories of India and an orphanage would know they were adopted and have experience of their birth country. A baby would have to be brought up to understand why he or she had been adopted, to appreciate the natural mother's dilemma and to respect her for her decision. This would be hard enough; but to help them understand why their native country also could not care for them and yet help them know and love that country would be a special responsibility. I began to realize that when you adopt from abroad, you adopt the country as well as the child.

This focus on India reminded me of my mother, a history lecturer who so admired the country with its seventeen languages and eight official religions, with people of such beauty who exude an inner peace and patience with life so unlike the West. She had always wanted to visit India and would have loved to have accompanied me there, where she would probably have kissed the ground at the Gandhi memorial had she lived long enough to do so. Whether or not through her influence, I have always found it easy to make friends with Asians and have kept in touch with friends in Australia and the USA as well as London and Delhi. Twelve years ago, when I decided to foster a child through ActionAid, it was an Indian child that I requested. To adopt India as well as the child would be a privilege; and so it has proved to be. Having a real link to a well-loved country is an enriching experience; when something happens there – good or bad – you feel it happens to you as well.

I felt this adoption was right for me, and wrote to Marilyn to say that adopting a baby would be wonderful and I'd appreciate any help she could give. By this time Lizzie was very enthusiastic about a baby since she was now doing a child-care course in school and a *real* baby would give her an advantage in writing essays! Once I felt that I'd made the right decision, which had taken many months, that seemed like the end of the journey, but of course it was only the beginning. How to go about it? Marilyn was immediately helpful and set the ball rolling by going to see the doctor on my behalf, telling her about me and my situation. The doctor is quite protective towards her babies because they are born to very young unmarried girls who come to her knowing she will be able to have them adopted abroad as opposed to going to an overcrowded orphanage. The girls come from many parts of Northern India, usually brought by their parents who were very anxious about the social consequences of an unmarried girl of 16 years or so being pregnant. Many parents and girls request an abortion; however, most are at least six months pregnant and it is too late. Once the doctor convinces them not to seek an abortion elsewhere, because of the danger to the girl, she invites them to remain in the hospital for the remainder of their pregnancy, doing their own cooking, supplying their own bedding, etc. They do not see the baby when it is born; this is her policy. She makes sure they are sedated immediately before the birth, and most ask to go home that day if possible. They desperately want to get back to a normal life after their 'visit to relatives in Delhi'.

One month after my letter to Marilyn, the doctor had 'accepted' me; the lawyer had as well, and I was told there were several babies due and young girls anxious to return home. Marilyn would be able to send all the appropriate papers for the Indian adoption once the baby was born; however, what was required at this end? Without a UK agency for overseas adoption the situation is very confusing, in fact it's chaotic. You talk to everyone you know who knows someone who has adopted abroad, you network outward and come up with many conflicting pieces of advice about how to prepare for the British adoption, how to get entry clearance as well as how to process the papers from abroad once they arrive. Through contacts in Parent to Parent Information on Adoption Services (PPIAS) and the National Association for the Childless (NAC) I talked to people who had adopted from Mexico, Thailand, Columbia, Chile and Peru; needless to say, everyone had done it differently, some as long ago as six years, and things can change quickly in these developing countries. The founder of NAC, Peter Houghton, put me in touch with key people at the DHSS, who made it clear that their views were generally unsupportive towards inter-country adoption (ICA). The Home Office sent me their standard letter on the process of ICA – this was in 1983 and before the plain English version came out, and it did little to enlighten me. My local authority hadn't a clue at the time, but to my surprise the head of adoption and fostering wished me well and also wrote a note of congratulation once I came home with the baby. She was not in favour of the new 'colour-coding' policy being practised in adoption and unfortunately retired soon after. Another seven 'friends of friends' friends' who had adopted abroad all gave good advice. Eventually I had gained the advice of five lawyers with experience in this field and twelve adoptive parents from all over the UK. I had spoken to three stern government officials and must have owned at least ten shares in British Telecom before privatization.

It was never clear what papers the British authorities needed for my entry into the UK with a baby from India. (By 1987, when I was adopting my second baby, there were specific papers that a lawyer friend obtained for me.) Marilyn rang several times to see how things were going. Finally I was able to tell her that there was a process for entering Britain with an adopted baby, but I was beginning to realize that it was more of a theory than a process.

It was the beginning of October, the leaves had fallen, and Lizzie and I were tidying up the garden when the telephone rang. It was Marilyn, saying how glad she was that there did seem to be a way through to adopting and returning home with a baby, and she had informed the lawyer and the doctor; I thanked her. 'The doctor wanted me to ring you to say she has a baby boy and a baby girl, both two weeks old.' 'That's nice,' I said pleasantly, passing the time of day, 'she must be busy'. A long pause. 'She wanted *you* to be the first to know.' Then a very long pause. The penny finally dropped, I couldn't believe this moment was real. I was to choose a baby 12,000 miles away. In a strained voice I whispered, 'I'd like to adopt the little boy and please call him Joshua'. With relief in her voice that I'd finally come around, she rang off with the words, 'I'll send you the papers right away'. I had been expecting to be offered only a girl and not a choice, since I'd been led to believe that boys rather than girls were usually adopted by Indian couples, because of the dowry system. But the truth was that I had been fantasizing about my *ideal* family – a boy and *then* a girl – and had always felt that if possible the boy should be older, especially as I had been the eldest followed by two boys. When you're 16 years old, brothers of 13 and 10 years old, and their friends, are not very interesting.

But where had the name Joshua come from?

It emerged as I thought about adopting a baby from India and the types of names I associated with the country – Jaquish, Jadeep and Jog were names of Indian men I had met professionally at various marketing conferences abroad; a name starting 'Ja' seemed right somehow. Jack? No. John? No. Jason? No. And there it was, Joshua. Even better Joshua was different, not so common. How wrong I was! In every class, toddler or playgroup he's been in, no matter how small the group, there's always been another Joshua. At the playground the mothers call out a refrain of 'Joshuas'.

I still couldn't believe it would all happen. The papers arrived quickly from India – it never took more than four days for the post – and the telephone became a hotline. I had to find a notary, obtain my accountant's statement of my affairs and the doctor's report, and determine the times for visiting the Foreign and Commonwealth Office and the Indian High Commission for the relevant legalization and stamping of the documents. More time was spent on the telephone to Westminster Social Services asking for a copy of my home study to be sent to India, the one done for Lizzie's fostering. They didn't know their position concerning inter-country adoption and I had to keep calling; finally they said they would send it if a social worker in India requested it. The hospital social worker in India looked over my papers, talked to the doctor and immediately wrote the letter making the request. More calls to Westminster: they agreed in principle but so-and-so was on leave and had to approve, and then they had to make a copy and it was sixteen pages long. I offered to make the copy for them; no, I was not allowed to see it! (I finally *did* see it when the lawyer in India gave me a copy once all the papers had gone through. Today, most London social services departments have an open policy about their reports, but this was 1983.) I think they got fed up with my telephone calls, or was it because my adoption officer in Haringey told me the name of the boss at Westminster? It took them four weeks to take my home study from the file, get one signature, xerox the sixteen pages, put it in an envelope and stamp it. Meanwhile, all the other papers had been notarized and despatched to Delhi: medical;

accountant; verification of employment status; letter approving the adoption; statement of intent to adopt; letter giving the Delhi lawyer Power of Attorney, and the adoption questionnaire.

Thank goodness for Marilyn, who rang often and wrote as well to report what was going on. She and the lawyer had looked into the issue of an entry visa and had learned from other English people there that it would probably take four to five months. I had wanted it all to be done properly, entry visa and all, but it was not to be. Joshua was in an overcrowded baby nursery; at one month he'd had bronchitis; he needed to come home. Lawyers who had also adopted assured me that as long as I had all the papers required to apply for the visa plus Joshua's adoption papers and passport, no baby had ever been turned back yet, and the government was not keen to be seen doing so. I patched together papers which the three different lawyers I knew said were essential: health and accountant's reports, and a statement from the doctor that the baby had been abandoned at birth and that he was a normal, healthy baby. Then one contact pointed out that my West-minster home study was two years old and that we should get an interim one to cover that time; a lawyer friend agreed and recom-mended a very experienced social worker who came to see Lizzie and me for an afternoon. She basically focused on Lizzie and our lifestyle, and my vocational situation. Her three-page report was added on to my package, which I then also had notarized just in case.

At the beginning of November, Marilyn called to say that the papers seemed to be in order and she would take them to the lawyer immedi-ately, as he was anxious to press on because he wanted to get into the court before the Christmas recess. That evening she was also going over to the hospital to see Joshua again; he was now 6 weeks old. Five days later I got the most lovely letter from her with my baby's picture in it. She apologized for the photograph, which failed to reveal his lovely dimples and his wonderful, big, round, dark eyes which were closed because of the camera's flash. Well, he looked like a baby, and his head was a nice shape; that was reassuring. What a lovely note she wrote saying how beautiful he was now and that he was smiling and how pleased the doctor was that I would have him. She was also most reassuring about the Indian lawyer who was very committed; he and his wife had only one child and yearned for more. She added that she realized I was so far away, and having to put trust in people I did not know in order to adopt my baby must be difficult. I was so grateful for her sensitivity that I immediately rushed out and bought big stuffed polar bears for her two little girls. These took up one entire suitcase on the outward plane journey.

Another wonderful moment – 29 November – the telephone rang. 'It's gone through the court, you are now the legal "guardian" of Joshua. The lawyer is very pleased that he will get the passport in ten days.' It had actually happened! Guardianship is the only way to 'adopt' in India, due to the influence of the Muslim religion which does not recognize adoption. Of course, Marilyn wanted to know when I would be there. Now I needed a visa and had to go to the Indian High Commission to obtain it. There was lots of shopping for everyone in India: my good friends the Kumars and their children, and the doctor, had asked for things from Marks & Spencer for herself and her children. Then there was the shopping around for a reasonable flight to India, as this was the most popular time of year for Indians to visit their country. Fortunately, a friend who knows the airline business put me in touch with a very helpful group who usually deal only with Indians going home, but they were very positive about my adoption and found an excellent return package, leaving on 12 December. Lizzie helped me organize the baby's things, many of which were given by friends. The support was wonderful. We finished our Christmas shopping and prepared the house. Lizzie sent out her Christmas cards: she was nearly 14 years old and had to have the right card for the right person. I addressed my cards and typed up a special letter to be duplicated upon my return, *if* everything went well. It described all of Lizzie's activities to update our friends, and announced Joshua's arrival, thanked everyone for their help and moral support, and hoped those abroad would come and see us as we weren't going to be very mobile for a while. My Christmas cards and letter would be very late that year, especially those to Australia and New Zealand, because I wasn't due back in London until 21 December and daren't send them until we were safely back and he was really home – it might be bad luck.

The day came to fly to Delhi; we carried Lizzie's suitcase across the street to our friends, then we reviewed what gifts she wanted from India, especially a black rectangular bag for school-books and something made of leather for her father.

It was an exciting, anxious and sobering flight to India. I was now the mother of a tiny baby on my way to collect him. I had somehow been entrusted by destiny to bring him to maturity, prepare him for his adult life, guide him, support him and, most important of all, just *be there* for him. What would he be like? What would the hospital be like, the doctor? And Marilyn; could I ever express my gratitude to her?

After the overnight flight, my friend Dr Kumar met me at the airport, where we made a quick call to the doctor who wanted me to come to the hospital when she finished her clinic at 1 p.m. It was now 11 a.m., 13 December. It was lovely to have lunch with all the Kumars and catch up, but I must admit that my mind was elsewhere. Here I was in Delhi and so was my son, with whom I would spend the rest of my life, and someone else was feeding him his lunch. He felt so close and yet so far.

Finally I could prepare to go to the hospital nursery. I got out the little stuffed seal I'd bought him, which eventually became known as Gee-Gee and goes everywhere with him. I wanted something to present to him and something to put on him. I realized a new territorial feeling of wanting to make him mine. So I took along his baby-sling for him to try on and let him get used to.

Dr Kumar put me into a bone-shaking, three-wheeled taxi; they always feel a bit top-heavy, which is quite worrying when they 'slalom' between lorries, ox carts, buses, sauntering cows, coaches, bicycles, cars of all sizes, motorbikes, dust carts and tricycles. I arrived intact and was taken to the doctor's home; she, like other doctors, lives in the hospital compound. I briefly met her daughter, son and husband and then was taken over to meet Joshua. After removing our shoes we walked into the nursery, which was stiflingly hot because all the newborns are brought here. The three *ayahs* (nannies) were sitting in a row bottle-feeding some of the babies. 'Yours is over here,' she said and walked towards some tiny cribs against the wall. 'Joshua, your Mama is here', were the last words I remember hearing. I looked down on this little bundle, and little he was, only nine pounds at three months; a friend had recently had a baby that was nine pounds at birth. He was swathed rather than dressed and he was looking blankly up at the ceiling. Nothing in the room had colour; the *ayahs* were all in beige, the bedding and wrappings on the babies were all beige and white, as were the walls and ceiling. The only colour was the green stripe on a towel hung near the tap next to the door so that the doctors could wash and dry their hands when they entered.

I picked him up and held him. Slowly he turned his gaze towards me and our eyes met. 'So you are going to grow up with me as your mother', I whispered to him. He seemed to look puzzled but decided to snuggle up anyway, and he felt ever so cuddly and loving, and that is how he has remained even now at the boisterous 6-year-old phase, where he throws himself about physically and emotionally as he discovers his strength and power.

I've often been asked, what were your feelings when you met him for the first time? There were so many feelings: joy; anxiety – will I be all right as a Mum?; sadness to have waited so long for a baby; gratitude to the young girl who did not run off to an abortionist, but stayed to have this lovely baby; confusion – what do I do first for him?; relief to have got this far; fearful about getting him back into Britain and obtaining the British adoption order. As I sat with the *ayahs* and fed him I was overwhelmed by the realization that I had walked into this room a childless foster mother and now I was feeding my baby, I was beginning to experience motherhood. After his feed I put him in the sling and walked out into the garden. The movement put him to sleep and when we returned to the nursery and I laid him down, his big, round, brown eyes met mine for that 'moment of recognition' natural mothers experience when they and their babies look deep into each other's souls and feel bonded for life. It was as though he was saying, 'So you are finally here, so I do have a mother', and I was saying, 'So I've found you at last'. The next day when I came in the doctor and I chatted as we stood next to his cot. He started to cry. 'Oh', she said, 'he wants you to pick him up'. He did seem to want to join in the conversation and snuggled up again; yes, this feels like my baby, I heard myself thinking.

Over the next few days I fed, changed and played with him, and collected his papers from the lawyer and the doctor, paying the lawyer £300 for legal, court and passport fees and the doctor £3 per day for the ninety days of his stay in the hospital. I was invited to her home for lunch. She showed me her 'baby book' – twenty babies who had gone to various Western countries from her clinic over the last three years (we are all asked to send at least two letters and pictures each year, which I've enjoyed doing). I also visited Marilyn – to thank her and to get to know this very generous person and her two children, by then 2 and 4 years of age. They all came to visit us a year later in London.

There was a lot of Christmas shopping to do, especially for Lizzie, and presents to deliver to the Kumars. I spent a day going to visit the Taj Mahal and Fatchpur Sikri, a sixteenth-century deserted city, and a morning seeing old Delhi; the old town is fascinating. The Raj Ghat (memorial to Ghandi) was a place of peace and beauty, but I always spent at least four hours a day with Joshua.

One week later, at 2 a.m. we were in a taxi leaving the hospital compound for the airport; many *ayahs* and nurses were at the gate waving goodbye to us. We were off to London – the journey that would dramatically change both our lives. Joshua will not be an orphan sent to a large institution in Delhi where he would have no last name, no birthday remembrance, little if any education, no chance to fulfil his human potential (as it happens he has a fine singing voice, a lovely aesthetic sense of colour, texture and design and an avid interest in wildlife, all of which give him great personal pleasure). In an institution he would not be part of his own culture but rather *set apart* from it. Without a family, community or neighbourhood to be part of he would never develop more than a vague sense of his own identity. And at the age of 7 he would have to leave custodial care and fend for himself in some form of 'cardboard city'. We've all seen pictures of the vacant gazes of unwanted street urchins or those in crowded custodial care. Being wanted, respected, encouraged, supported, loved and a *part* of the life around you brings out the real person so promising at birth. And I believe it is the most essential basic right. As for me, I had always wanted to be a mother and share my life with a child, going through all the stages of development with them, being there for them and just being part of evolution – a link between my past and the next generation.

As Joshua slept on the plane I wondered about his mother; I was told she was a schoolgirl of about sixteen from a village further south, whose parents brought her to Delhi to be out of the gaze of the community. An illegitimate child in her culture was totally unacceptable, and according to the doctor, all the young girls plead for a termination so they can go home as quickly as possible. She finds it essential to give them basic sex education to avoid the same thing happening again.

Every birthday I wonder if she thinks of him (or 'it'); she never saw him and never asked what sex the baby was. It sounded as if the birth was a 'getting it over with': the solution to an unfortunate problem or a punishment for making a mistake and shaming her family. If she does think of him I hope she feels she did the right thing, and I hope that eventually she finds a meaningful life as a wife and mother.

And what about the issue of bringing up an Asian child in London? We are lucky to be in one of the most racially-mixed communities in Britain – Haringey. Joshua constantly sees many people who look like him. We have a wide choice of schools; I chose the Rudolf Steiner because it instils a sense of stability in the children by focusing them on how they are an integral part of the rhythms of nature. They also explore things organically, including the alphabet, and they try to replace competition with co-operation at all ages. The ethnic mix is amazing; no two children are the same and the classes are small and the teachers very caring and creative. He's never had an unhappy day at his school in three years.

We've discussed his 'brownness' and my beigeness, as I am part Celtic, part American Indian, plus English, Scots and Irish. He has the most gorgeous orange-brown-toned skin with lovely dimples and bright, alert eyes and a winning smile and already four 'girlfriends'. But most of all, he likes colour and loves being called 'beautiful', which strangers do regularly. He may be in for some hurtful comments someday, aren't we all; I wore bands on all my front teeth from the age of 8 to 11 and was called everything under the sun, especially 'metal mouth'. One of my brothers was very clumsy and could trip crossing an empty room, and the other was very short; I saw their hurts and problems too. Joshua is now more concerned about his height and whether he can run faster than anything else. My thoughts on the plane were for a happy, loved, secure child, and I vowed I would do my best.

My next thoughts turned to Immigration and bringing him in without an entry visa. I wish I knew then what I know now; that the entry visa is not an absolute requirement, it's not a law but rather 'a preferred procedure' as stated in the Home Office document. However, it has grown over the years into a very strong 'habit'.

Unfortunately for us, we got a young immigration official who was new to the job; he called in all his superiors and soon we had a posse of immigration officers and the entire area to ourselves, despite the fact that it was four days before Christmas. I felt very isolated and victimized, sitting there after a twelve-hour flight being grilled about why I had not gone through the system for an entry visa. I kept repeating that other adopters and specialist lawyers had assured me that I was entitled to a three-month visa upon production of his adoption papers, since the British Consulate in Delhi was in no position to handle visas quickly. Furthermore, my son, now aged three months, was no longer able to stay in a newborns nursery; it was essential for him to come home. I added that my MP was aware that I was coming into the country and would request the usual twenty-eight-day visa if we called him. They went away with all my papers, then came back and asked if we wanted sandwiches or a bed to have a rest. I refused everything but a place to change Joshua, saying we had to go soon as we were being met by someone. More stern looks; they came back to ask various questions about why I had all the papers to submit for the visa and I explained that my private social worker and a lawyer specializing in adoption had advised me to have these papers ready for the eventual adoption here. Another hour went by and I had to call my friend to tell her where we were. I asked the officials when she could come back to collect us. They were unsure. No one was actually hostile, but the army of immigration officials we had collected were certainly all busy acting out their disapproval of people without the right papers. Since it was lunchtime it might have been a problem for them to get through to the Home Office, who grant the entry visas, but they could have given the reason for the hold-up. More stern looks; all the time I kept repeating to myself what everyone had told me: 'they'd never sent a baby back yet'. But couldn't they insist? My passport is American although I've been a permanent resident since 1973; could they decide that this case was different? When official-dom holds all the cards the feeling of helplessness is inevitable.

My friend Renee had decided to come back to Heathrow at 1.30 p.m.; she's the eternal optimist who felt that if we were in the country, what more could they say. In the end she was right. Not long after 1.30 p.m. they brought back my papers, having made copies. However, they kept Joshua's passport and instead presented me with a paper demanding that after twenty-eight days we return to Heath-row with his baggage unless a 'visa' was granted in that time. This time a very nice lady, who even managed a smile, gave me some advice about what to do next to apply for the visa extension.

Home at last, and reunion with Lizzie and many friends and neigh-bours who came to see this little bundle, who by that time was very out of sorts – hungry, smelly and tired. Bath, bottle and cuddle, and he and Gee-Gee were off to sleep in his special little crib.

The next day I was back on the telephone to various lawyers, one of whom wanted me to pay him £3,000 to make Joshua a ward of court! A more reasonable suggestion was to get a very experienced lawyer to write a letter to the Home Office backing up my application for a visa and pointing out that Joshua was my son and legal responsibility in the eyes of his native country. It was a beautifully written letter; very persuasive and thorough. However, it was too late to be needed: the day the final draft was to be typed I got a call from the very nice lady at Immigration who said, 'You've got your visa and no need to pay any attention to the paper demanding your return to Heathrow; sorry you were given such a bad time here, and best of luck to you'. What a lovely moment. The next day his passport arrived with a six-month visa stamp dated 23 January 1984.

From then on things went very smoothly with the British adoption. We had a sweet young social worker who came to see us four times and prepared a very thorough report for the court. She was quite fascinated with the idea of inter-country adoption, as it was something she would consider for herself in later years, she explained. She did get cold feet at the end and deferred our court date by a month once she heard that a judge at our court – Clerkenwell Magistrates – had demanded that a natural mother be found somewhere in Venezuela to sign a form giving her consent to the adoption of her baby at least six weeks after the birth, which is the practice in England. The International Social Services had spent a month without tracing her and my social worker was anxious to strengthen her argument that Joshua had been abandoned by a young girl, who probably did not give her true name, and who had disappeared back into her elusive village where she would be most upset to be found and asked to sign a paper in front of her community. The doctor in India sent another note confirming that the mother had never seen the baby and had left very quickly after the birth, effectively abandoning him. This was also stated on his birth certificate.

Our day came: 9 July 1984. My social worker was more anxious than I was; and when she saw that our judge was Asian she was very concerned. Later she told me this was because of my single status, would he approve? But more importantly, would he feel negative about bringing a child from India to live in the West? On the contrary, he was beaming as he said, 'I have read your papers and they are all in order', (looking at Joshua), 'you are a very lucky little boy and I can see that you are well loved. I wish you every happiness'. It all took two minutes and we both walked out in tears with Joshua looking quizzically at both of us. Friends came over with the champagne that evening, the social worker joined us, and it was a lovely feeling to know it was all over.

It was to be more than four years before I would be back at Clerkenwell Court in the same judge's chambers, with a different judge presiding over the proceedings for Sophia's adoption. She was 2 years old by then; Joshua had been 10 months. One might have been safe in assuming that the second adoption would be easier, after all you know what to expect, you have all the papers, they need updating. However, as Victor Hugo said, 'Truth is rarely pure and never simple'.

In the three years between Joshua's and Sophia's adoptions there had been a number of changes in India. First of all, nothing could commence until the baby was 3 months old, and I had a new Indian lawyer, and a very anxious one at that, due to his inexperience. He immediately registered her birth date for one month *earlier* than it actually was to give him more lead time. This has become a real problem over the years as it is the date on her passport. The papers from India had more requirements to fulfil. The one that rather amused me asked you to send photos of every room in your house. A friend laughingly suggested that I buy a set of postcards of Kensington

Palace! Every paper that I sent the new lawyer did not suit him; when I talked to him on the phone he was extremely anxious and full of stories about all the work he was doing on my behalf; yet nothing happened.

Finally, when Sophia was 5 months old (6 months according to the lawyer's registration of her birth) the London lawyer, who had written the very impressive letter to the Home Office about Joshua's visa in 1984, wrote to the lawyer in India, more or less telling him to get on with it as he had the best documentation that could be supplied, given the fact that Britain does not have an agency for inter-country adoption, which he constantly complained about. Furthermore, she pointed out to him that the same court had approved me as a 'guardian' for Joshua three-and-a-half years ago which was followed by approval for adoption in the British court three years ago. There was the Westminster home study, the home study covering Joshua's adoption by Haringey, a private social worker's home study covering the time gap of two-and-a-half-years after the Haringey one was conducted. She ended by stating that he should be glad he had such an easy case to deal with. A month later he had the Indian adoption (guardianship) complete and the passport ready. Meanwhile, I was trying to do it properly this time by getting an entry visa (because of new legislation applying to India), and even ringing the British Consulate in Delhi several times, involving my MP, Hugh Rossi, who was very supportive, the Director of Social Services for Haringey, plus the Leader of the Council, who were equally supportive in requesting that my papers should be accepted by the DSS (as it now is) and the Home Office. There was always something 'not quite right'. As one tired civil servant said to me, 'It's the fashion now not to promote inter-racial or inter-country adoptions; in another six to eight years the fashion will change'. He was so right, but that didn't help Sophia in 1987. What to do? I was told it could be another six months. I couldn't bear the thought of my dear little girl reaching the age of 9 months and still being institutionalized. As a psychologist I'd read a lot about separation, bonding and the 'fear of strangers' phenomenon that sets in when babies are 8 or 9 months old. Now I was getting anxious that we would lose her babyhood and that I would be a stranger to her and lose our chance for a close bond.

Then a letter arrived from the doctor in Delhi: 'Sophia is getting too big for my baby nursery, she needs to come home now; she also does not like the heat' – it was June and 105° in Delhi – 'and has gone off her food. What is wrong, why does it take so long?'

While the various groups in London involved in approving entry visas passed my papers round and round, and I followed them by phone from the Home Office to Haringey to the DSS and painfully slowly back round again, Sophia was lying in a hot nursery in Delhi. The annoying thing was that they were always reassuring me that they had the child's best interests at heart. Such nonsense. The system was more important than the person. Eventually I lost heart with the system and felt something had to be done. I called the doctor in India again and asked her to send me a letter with the word *urgent* on top and to follow it up with another letter in two or three days' time. She heartily agreed. Meanwhile, I shopped around for a reasonable flight to Delhi, but again I had picked a very busy and expensive time of year. I stopped calling everyone about Sophia's papers, including my very supportive MP, organized the domestic situation, got all the baby things out and left for India on 26 June with a return booked for 1 July. As it was for such a short time I stayed in the hospital compound in part of the doctor's house. The next day I once again walked into the baby nursery with the doctor, where all the babies were lying on mats on the floor because of the heat (now 114°). She went over to a little sleeping bundle – 'Your Mama is here, Sophia, Mama' – and the little eyes opened and looked me over as if to say 'where have you been?' I picked her up and she felt so good, so natural. She was gorgeous. Thank goodness I was taking her home. She clung to me and we walked over to a swing in the garden. She sat on my lap and then fell asleep. We ate, bathed, watched television and shopped together. After three days we felt right as mother and daughter.

On 1 July, again at 2 a.m., we left the compound together in a taxi with even more people to wave us off because the children in the compound often played with the older babies in the nursery. They were all there!

Now for the tricky part – getting on the plane and through Immigration in London. Because of new legislation specifying entry visas for Asians entering Britain, Air India required those without one to sign a paper stating they would take full responsibility if turned back in Britain. A patient of Dr Kumar's was an executive with Air India; he said someone at the airport would help me with this. I was to ask for his deputy, Mr C, to sign the paper regarding Sophia and me. I went to the first-class check-in desk as they were the least busy, and asked for Mr C. I don't know who he was but he must have been very important. No one asked why I wanted to see him; they just whisked me through formalities and on to first class (with my tourist class ticket) and we were off to London! I said nothing and Sophia looked lovely in her beautiful colour-coordinated first-class baby cot.

Perhaps, I thought, this is a good omen for Sophia – she will land on her feet wherever she goes, and how true it's been. She's a wily charmer with a winning smile, who stands her ground and comes up trumps every time.

We entered Immigration at Heathrow and the whole horrible experience with Joshua came back. I chose a nice-looking young woman to approach, but when I handed her my papers the strain hit me and I dissolved into tears. Must we go through this again, being held at Immigration and made to feel a common criminal? I wasn't bringing in drugs, I was bringing a precious, very much wanted child of 8-and-a-half months, my child according to India. She was very kind, yet efficient, enquiring whether I had been asked for my visa in Delhi. 'No', I said. 'Strange', she replied, and I thanked the unknown Mr C. When she saw the doctor's two letters she said 'Oh no, no wonder you are upset, I'm sure we can work something out'. The two letters were brief; the first was to the effect that the doctor could no longer keep Sophia in the nursery, she was now too big and they needed the space, so she would have to go to an orphanage. The second letter was dated a few days later: 'The orphanage cannot take your daughter because she has been adopted by you, she is not an orphan and under Indian law she cannot stay in an orphanage'.

The doctor and I had taken a calculated risk; we had put her in limbo, made her homeless, thus giving Immigration a *reason* to let her stay. They agreed to let her in for two weeks while they studied all the papers now with the Home Office, where they'd been for two months. The very next day they approved the papers and sent her passport back with a three-month visa. We had made it again, but I don't feel I could ever face it another time. The anxiety and the uncertainty is quite unbearable. Sophia's adoption had taken five weeks of my working time, Joshua's one. I work as a freelance consultant, so this was very stressful. My telephone bill for the adoption was £400, and the inexperienced Indian lawyer nearly doubled the fee by wasting time. It also took longer for her British adoption because the law had changed here as well; now the baby has to live with you for at least a year before you can go to court. My social worker for this adoption was head of the Haringey adoption and fostering unit and a very busy lady; her report took longer, so we didn't get to the court until November 1988. Another addition to British adoption procedure was the meetings with the guardian *ad litem* appointed to represent the interests of the child as she was, like Joshua, an abandoned baby at birth. He visited us twice and also wrote a report which this time did *not* include Lizzie who was now 19 years old, and living in her own flat in the West End of London and working with a travel firm. Not that she isn't part of the family. She stays with us often and visits too – the children love her and she adores them.

The final hurdle to completing the family took place on 18 November 1988, when Sophia, Joshua, myself and our lovely au pair from Austria, one of the children's guardians, our social worker *and* the guardian *ad litem* attended the judge's chambers. As the seven of us were seating ourselves he was already starting his brief comments – 'I have looked at the papers and they all seem. . .'. Suddenly, he looked up and noticed that an audience had assembled. He began again, feeling that such a gathering deserved more attention than he had planned. Smiling kindly, he said, 'It's nice of you all to come, perhaps you could introduce me'. Formalities completed he then allowed himself the indulgence of an informal chat. He complimented the social worker and the guardian *ad litem* on their excellent reports and complimented the au pair on her role, as well as the children's guardian. He then turned to the children and asked Joshua if he liked having a little sister. With a twinkle in his eye and flashing both dimples Joshua said, 'Yes, her name is Sophia', as though he was helping the judge out with some vital information.

He greeted 2-year-old Sophia and turned to me. 'You have, of course, been approved as an adoptive mother in this court once before, and it has obviously been a success. I am very pleased to approve the adoption of little Sophia.' He then looked rather more serious. 'Am I to assume that the family is now complete?' And, with his kindly smile returning, 'When we get to middle age we realize "tempus fugit", don't we?'; and he chuckled kindly.

I chuckled too and felt I couldn't have put it better myself. Yes, the family was definitely complete, my two lovely children each had a soul mate for life: someone born at the same hospital, with the same doctor attending, cared for by some of the same *ayahs*, both abandoned by a young, single girl who left very quickly after the birth without naming them. And miraculously they both adore each other and enjoy playing and chatting for hours. Somehow they seem to know they are special to each other. Perhaps its part of the phenomenon that midwives have observed for years – that adopted babies in any hospital nursery seem to know there's something special about them, they stand out, they shine. Joshua and Sophia, I believe, recognize this in each other.

Sophia, now 3 years old, participates in her own story:

MAMA   On 15 October 1986, a beautiful baby girl was born.
SOPHIA Named Sophia.

MAMA	Mama quickly got all the papers together to send to India.
SOPHIA	And you sent me brown bear [a favourite small teddy] and a book about brown bear, see, here they are.
MAMA	Yes, that's right. And, then Mama flew to Delhi and went quickly to the hospital nursery.
SOPHIA	And when you came in I was sound asleep on mats on the floor because it was very hot, and you woke me up and we went out to that − what was it?
MAMA	The swing in the garden, darling.
SOPHIA	And then we came home on the aeroplane and got in Renee's car and went to pick up Joshua at Mary's house and then we all came home.

And since then we have tried to live happily ever after.

I would like C. P. Snow to have the last word. It's a saying I cut out twenty years ago and kept for the right time in my life: 'A measure of what you *really* want in life is what *happens* to you'.

7 Eventually . . . and so to Sri Lanka

Audrey and David Wilson

David and Audrey married sixteen years ago and, being Catholics, awaited their first pregnancy as a matter of course. Since they both wanted children, they accepted the Church's teaching on contraception without question. Audrey tells their story.

It didn't really matter if I became pregnant straight away, or after several months. A pregnancy would definitely be achieved – we never questioned that we would experience problems having children.

After two years there was no sign of a pregnancy, and as I was experiencing some pain on intercourse I was referred for investigation to a local hospital. The cause of both complaints was attributed to a tilted womb, which was corrected on a day-care basis. Another two years later and still no pregnancy. This time our GP referred us to an infertility clinic where investigations revealed that both Fallopian tubes were blocked, twisted, scarred and covered in adhesions. Not good news, to say the least – no wonder we had not achieved a pregnancy in four years.

Microsurgery was our only hope, but even that had a low success rate where the damage was as great as ours. The consultant, however, believed that it was worth operating as this appeared to be our only chance of becoming genetic parents. At this point we felt that we had plenty of time on our side before we considered adoption – we were 28 and 32 years old respectively.

Two years after the microsurgery we were informed that the Fallopian tubes had become blocked again. We knew that *in vitro* fertilization (IVF) had been pioneered, but we didn't have the money to go privately. Anyway, there was a possibility that the hospital would pilot a research IVF programme in the near future. We contented ourselves with knowing that everything that could possibly be done for us had been done. We talked about our desire for a family, and reasoned that parenting was more important to us than having our own genetic child, so we applied to adopt. In our area all adoptions of children under the age of two are conducted by an adoption agency and not by the Department of Social Services. Their procedure involved selecting a certain number of couples only once a year from all applications. After two years of applying we were no further forward to becoming parents. An interview with the agency led us to believe that certain factors were operating against us – our occupation ('young mothers have negative views of secondary teachers'), our religion ('most young mothers couldn't care less which religion their child is brought up in – that is, except Catholic or Mormon'), and our age (now 30 and 34 years old, with an upper limit of 35). There was no point in our applying to the Catholic adoption agency in our area, as its lists had been closed for six years (some years later, through our involvement with NAC, we discovered that this was not entirely true, as they operated a policy of opening and closing their lists without telling anyone, so it was 'pot luck' when you phoned!).

Back home again we talked through our desire for a family, and again we admitted that parenting was important to us. There were children older than 2 years who needed parenting. We approached the adoption agency and began assessment for a family of two or three children up to the age of 7 years. We attended adoption clubs, children's discos and group meetings. When our assessment was nearing completion, we heard from the Infirmary. They were starting their IVF research programme and we were ideal candidates. Did we wish to be considered? A consultation made us aware of the extremely low success rate, and the likelihood that we would end our three attempts without achieving a pregnancy. On balance we decided that it was worth trying, admitting that we would never rest at ease if we refused the opportunity. Being honest individuals, we told our social worker (as home visits would inevitably clash with hospital stays), and were informed that our assessment would cease immediately. We had not come to terms with our infertility as we were re-entering treatment. It is difficult to explain how we felt on hearing that statement: undermined, cheated, and shattered were some of the emotions that rushed into our private world. We didn't expect the IVF to work but the social worker wouldn't listen. 'Come back to us when you've finally put treatment behind you', she said. Little did she realize the lack of understanding that this phrase exhibited for childless couples.

The consultant was correct. Three IVF attempts later, and still we had not achieved a pregnancy. The option existed to return to the adoption agency to complete our assessment for older children, but we could not in all honesty give an assurance that we would never re-enter treatment, and our consciences would not permit us to lie. The road ahead became one of life without children, or saving for IVF privately. We chose the latter.

Pregnancy came no nearer to us through paying for IVF. We underwent many attempts, including frozen embryos. We always got large numbers of eggs, most of which fertilized and divided, but never a pregnancy. The clinic we attended was baffled. They tried everything – varied the drugs, sent our culture medium for analysis, asked us to check that there was no scarring of the womb and suggested extensive hormone analysis (we managed to obtain both of the latter on the NHS locally). No one could come up with an answer. Believing that IVF would eventually produce our much desired family, and having ruled out surrogacy, we persevered, saving for each attempt and meeting the disappointment of each failure with renewed optimism (and overtime, through David's plumbing occupation) for the next attempt. Throughout those four years of IVF treatment we knew nothing about adopting from abroad. Living in Scotland, as we do, very few people have adopted through this method, and it is not as 'public' as it is in some parts of the UK.

In response to an article we wrote in the NAC Magazine three years ago about our IVF failures, experiences of adoption procedures in this country, and our probable future without children unless we persevered with IVF, a couple who had adopted from El Salvador contacted us and planted the seed of adopting from abroad.

We visited the couple and were introduced to various issues we would have to discuss – primarily the issue of 'Is it right to do this?' We talked at length about the problems of different cultures, the amount of prejudice the child would face, and our motives for adopting from abroad. Many nights of long conversations stretched into several months of examining the pros and cons. Eventually, we realized that we had explored these issues before – when we had applied to adopt a mixed-race or black child in this country (only to be told that same-race adopters were preferred). We knew that we wanted to be parents, to fill our lives with caring for children, and giving them the love in abundance we had to give. The search to find a country willing to accept our application therefore began.

An early decision not to adopt via lawyer's contacts steered us in the direction of applying to orphanages and government child welfare departments. Many of the letters had to be translated, and, not knowing anyone who spoke fluent Spanish or Portuguese, we started paying the first of several hefty translation bills. The first positive reply came from Thailand. We only had to get the backing of our local Social Services Department to do the home study and our application would be processed. Several telephone calls later to Social Services brought the oral assurance that they would indeed conduct the home study. When we asked for this in writing, the reply shattered us. The local authority would not undertake the task, and suggested we contact two adoption agencies in our region. The Catholic agency refused to assess us for inter-country adoption unless we had a connection with the country (we didn't); the other would, at a cost of £1,400. We found this sum unacceptable – it was like paying for a child – and so gave up on Thailand. Five months had so far passed.

Sri Lanka looked a possibility although we would have to use the services of a Dutch intermediary. We forwarded our papers for perusal, minus a private home study yet to be organized. Two weeks later, word came back – the Sri Lankan Government had banned adoptions. Our despondency soon turned to optimism when a letter arrived from the Child Welfare Department in Nepal. They would accept our application with a private home study. The rush was on. Everything was organized, documents certified as original, legalized and taken to the Nepalese Embassy. A courier winged our application away. Two months later we received notification of our application, and various telephone calls to Nepal assured us that our case was proceeding well – until several months later we were informed by the Head of Department there that there were no children for foreign adoption. We were stunned. A year had now gone by, and we were no further forward. It was at this stage that contact with others who had adopted was much needed: 'Don't give up. Try another country'.

Two sources in Colombia responded positively to our enquiry, and we submitted an application (with documents duly translated) to the government adoption agency in Bogota on the recommendation of a friend who had gone there on business and visited the agency and several orphanages. An official at the agency assured him that our application would be in order, even though we couldn't get a statutory home study. True to its word, a month later the agency informed us that they would proceed with our application, and we were to send our home study report. The next communication from them again sent our systems into shock. Our application had been rejected as our home study was not official. There then followed months of our sending certified letters from our Social Services Department outlining post-placement procedure here, a similar statement from an Officer of the Court, various letters of recommendation, a curriculum vitae from our private social worker with notarized letters attesting to her qualifications, and a fee to have our documents retranslated by the official court translator. The responses from the agency were so erratic (one letter would say that our application had been successful, and the next that we had been rejected) that we decided to submit yet another application to an orphanage in Bolivia when we heard from friends that its lists had reopened.

Eighteen months had passed, and we were still no nearer to adopting a child. By now our friendly Notary was feeling guilty at having children, British Rail was making a fortune out of our frequent trips from Glasgow to London, and Berlitz translators were fully acquainted with the difficulties of adopting from abroad. Contacts who had successfully adopted tried to reassure us by saying that we simply hadn't any luck.

Our third application, duly documented, certified, translated, legalized and authenticated, now left the UK for Bolivia. Surely now it would be third time lucky. Our intermediary for Bolivia was a missionary who lived in Sweden (made known to us via our friends who had successfully adopted there). As we knew no one in Bolivia this contact proved invaluable. Unfortunately, we were instructed to send more documents as the government were now demanding more vetting – they required a letter from the Social Services outlining their role in post-adoption placement, and a letter from the police stating that we didn't have a criminal record. The latter would not have been possible without a policeman 'friend' who was given unofficial permission to write a character reference for us on police-headed notepaper. This did the trick. Exactly two-and-a-half years after our first application we were informed that the adoption tribunal had accepted our application. What wonderful news! We were told to expect the name of a child the first week in September – two months later. Ironically, at the same time we also received further communications from Colombia. One stated that our application there had been rejected again, and the other that it had been accepted completely and was being sent to an outlying region to be processed for the name of a child. It was just as well that our Bolivian application had finally been accepted, as we didn't know whether to laugh or cry about Colombia!

September came and went, and still no news from Bolivia. At the end of September our Swedish contact informed us that the new Government had banned adoptions, and a further telephone call to the British Consul in La Paz took the carpet from under our feet by informing us that there had been no foreign adoptions from Bolivia for a year. So much for 'Third time lucky'.

David and I hit rock-bottom. It seemed that our decision not to go through a lawyer, and pay the huge fees involved, had worked against us. Applying to government departments and orphanages would definitely have been fruitful (apart from bans) if we had been able to gain the co-operation of our local Social Services. As it was, our three applications had probably cost the price of a lawyer – a lawyer who initially we could not have afforded, or felt at ease with.

In October we heard through the grapevine that adoptions from Sri Lanka had reopened. After much soul-searching, we decided to submit our fourth and last application. All our documents had to be updated again, sent to the Dutch intermediary for his perusal, taken to a notary, legalized and taken to the Sri Lankan Embassy. Instead of dispatching our application by courier, this time the Embassy put them in their diplomatic mail bag. All we had to do then was wait.

By mid November we were given a date to fly – 20 January. After all our disappointments, we couldn't believe it, but 20 January quickly came round. We boarded a plane at Glasgow for Gatwick, and then a connecting flight to Colombo. The flight was thirteen hours long but we enjoyed every moment, knowing that soon we would return with our baby. At Colombo, our intermediary had arranged for us to be met and driven the long drive to a hotel which was near the British High Commission and the lawyer's office. The 'hanging-about' then began.

We were summoned to visit the lawyer who told us that we would probably be allocated a boy as she had handled nothing but boys for more than a month. This came as quite a shock, as we had both plucked up the courage to admit that we preferred a girl in our application and felt relieved that we had expressed a preference. However, when you long to be parents, does it matter if the child is a boy or a girl? We readjusted our thoughts and began to talk of a boy. (When you adopt from Sri Lanka, you are not always given the name of a child before you fly.) Again more waiting, and another visit to the lawyer. We would have to be prepared to stay for four weeks, perhaps longer. She had personal business to attend to which would remove her from legal practice for two weeks. Still no named baby? We enquired into when we would see our baby, but were simply told 'soon'. Various documents had to be signed at the lawyer's, giving her permission to file for a court hearing and getting access to birth records of the child. Again we waited.

The next summons we received, a few days later (it seemed like an eternity), was to meet our baby. She was beautiful (she: not a boy!). She was 6-and-a-half months old and gorgeous. We had been told to prepare ourselves for the fact that we would meet the natural mother, as her written consent and appearance in court was mandatory. However, we never considered that the mother might change her mind. How silly we were, as later the unthinkable happened − the baby's mother did indeed change her mind. Although we were stunned when the lawyer told us this, we talked the situation through to ease our pain and help us to cope with events. On reflection we were glad that we were dealing with a country where that could happen, and where the lawyer obviously had no influence on the mother's decision. The mother obviously did not feel at ease giving her child up, and would have said so in court when grilled by the judge. Instead of feeling sorry for ourselves, we felt great sympathy with the mother. We began to see the positive side to her decision − she wanted her child, we wouldn't have to cope with a baby used to its natural mother, and 'it wasn't meant'.

That same day we were summoned again, and introduced to an 18-day-old baby girl whose mother had intimated when pregnant that she could not keep the baby. Our baby was tiny; she weighed only 4 lbs; she was so small, yet very healthy, smiling and contented. Standing there, in awe of this little mite, we knew in our hearts that this would be 'our baby'. Tears rolled down my cheeks, with David telling me to be strong.

An interview was then arranged with the Social Services Commissioner. Sitting in the waiting area outside his office, we met a nun with a 5-and-a-half-month-old baby girl. The baby had been abandoned at the orphanage by her mother, and the nun was trying to facilitate her adoption by a French doctor. She explained to us that in Sri Lanka it was not easy to adopt an abandoned baby, as the mother's signature was needed. Twice, in vain, they had searched for the mother. The nun's purpose, therefore, in seeing the Commissioner was to persuade him to waive the requirement of this signature. Three-quarters-of-an-hour later she emerged − unsuccessful. She had been instructed to search again.

The interview was nerve-racking, but looking back it was more due to our tension than to the attitude of the Commissioner or to the contents of the interview itself. We knew that our baby's mother would also have an interview with this man, and probably had had other interviews with lesser officials in the Social Services prior to this stage.

Two days later a court hearing was arranged − miraculously before our lawyer's departure. For the very first time in three years this was a stroke of good fortune. Words cannot adequately describe the events in court, or our emotions. The atmosphere was tense as we waited with other adopters at the family court. The judge was pleasant but officious, and scrutinized our papers. We stood before him, terrified that he would reject our application – but no! We emerged approved adopters, with our very own daughter. Overcome with emotions, all sorts of emotions, and my vision blurred by tears, we climbed into a taxi and returned to our hotel. Our daughter was beautiful – wrapped in a tea-towel and wearing a faded, worn shirt that tied at the neck. We laid her down on the bed and stared at her, unable to speak. We then drew nearer and nearer to her, and shared in her gurgles of delight. She had ten fingers and ten toes – she was perfect.

David then had to leave us and go to the Sri Lankan Immigration Department to collect her passport. Armed with the necessary documentation, he set off and came back hours later. Fortune again shone on us – we then got seats on the next flight from Colombo to Gatwick. We now only had to get her entry visa. The next morning David set off at 6.30 a.m. to queue at the High Commission. Again he took with him the necessary documentation – birth certificate, medical report, adoption order, mother's affidavit, UK passport, etc. Many, many hours later he returned. We could go home – back to the UK. Poorer by £2,800 through trying to get our applications accepted by Nepal, Colombia and Bolivia and the £4,000 (all-inclusive) it cost to adopt from Sri Lanka; richer in our arms, minds and hearts. Parents at last!

When our connecting plane eventually landed at Glasgow, after a six-hour delay at Gatwick, we were met by David's sister and brother-in-law. Susan rushed towards us, her eyes filled with tears of joy. The tiny bundle that was our daughter was fast asleep, oblivious to all the excitement and emotion. It was only at that moment that we knew just how much our desire for a family was shared by our own families. My mother and father arrived minutes later, and joined in the wonderful welcome. Although our families knew of our infertility, adoption attempts in this country, and struggle to adopt from abroad, they had never enquired of our progress. Mistakenly, we had interpreted this as lack of interest, but we know now that it was their inability to deal with our situation and their genuine desire not to upset us by seeming inquisitive – they had known of our repeated failures and our continual struggle to become parents, and wondered how much pain we could take.

For weeks our home was never devoid of visitors, all of whom openly showed their delight at our daughter and joy for us as parents. We have been inundated with presents and good wishes. The support has been tremendous. Whenever we mention the difficulties that she will face in the future due to her different appearance, we are told again and again that no one who made her life difficult through prejudice was worthy of consideration. Of course we know that, and we know now who our true friends and supporters are, but we cannot ignore the comments that will be made and the actions to which she may be subjected. As a baby she is immune to these hurts, but we must face them now and learn how to cope with them. Who do we turn to for help? Recently, friends in a similar situation sought advice from a race counselling helpline, only to be told to report the incident. This is not the sort of advice our friends or ourselves need. We need to know what to say to people who utter prejudices against our children; we need to know how to handle the emotions of our children and ourselves. Thankfully we have a small number of friends who have adopted from Sri Lanka, and together we will find and give the support we all need.

Our daughter is now 4 months old, and in the next few months we will decide if we can try for a second adoption and, if so, when that should be. For the moment, we want to cherish our time with her, and allow our lives to adjust completely to having a family – for adjust we most certainly have had to do.

Would we repeat the awful pain of the last sixteen years of infertility treatment and experiences with adoption workers to reach our present situation? Obviously, if we were to live them again there are things we would change; and although we can't change the past with all its pain, with help from others we've learned to handle our pain and emerged as parents. Some days we shout at each other or shout at our daughter, for some days she cries non-stop. However, recalling life without her recalls a life we rejected. If the sixteen pain-filled years were needed to reach our daughter, then 'yes', we would live them again!

8 The empty nest

Karina and John Woodford

Karina and John both had a previous marriage. Karina takes up their story.

Infertility and adoption were things that happened to other people. An increasingly infrequent 'Adoption' notice under the Births column in *The Times* would be read with some wonder – I wonder why? I wonder how? – and then dismissed from thought. That was until four years ago, when we joined that hitherto unknown band of other people.

Johnny and I had both been married before and neither of us were in a great hurry to commit ourselves again too quickly. I had two children from my first marriage who lived with me in London, while Johnny was enjoying his newly found bachelorhood on his own in the country. He had not been as lucky as me: he also had two children, both of whom had died. His first baby was born prematurely and had not survived, but Nicola, his adored second child, was just 4 years old when she died of encephalitis. I can only imagine the pain he must have gone through; nothing can be worse than losing a child.

Eventually, ten years after we met (I mentioned we weren't in any hurry) we got married and I moved to the country with my children. Both of them were thrilled as they had always loved Johnny. After all, he had been around since they were 5 and 3 years old. The next most logical step for me was to give Johnny a child; it was something of paramount importance to me. I hadn't been prepared to have a baby before we married as I am rather old-fashioned and, having two impressionable teenagers on my hands, I felt that mother should at least try to set a good example. They were both delighted at the thought of a brother or sister but, being teenagers, were far more interested in acquiring new bicycles or worrying about the next lot of exams.

About a year passed and I still wasn't pregnant, and each month brought more disappointment. I wasn't unduly worried as I thought it might be my age – I was 40 years old – but I did think it was a little strange as I had always got pregnant so easily before. Eventually I made an appointment with my gynaecologist, who suggested I try some hormone pills. I went home full of excitement, convinced that the magic pills would do the trick. They didn't. Another visit to London and the gynaecologist said he would like me to go into the London Clinic for a couple of days to have a laparoscopy so that he could have a look around my inside for any possible problems.

The following week I checked in for the operation. When I had come round from the anaesthetic he told me that I had fairly bad endometriosis but that I wasn't to worry, it could be cleared up by very strong hormone pills which I would have to take for six months to a year, during which time I could not get pregnant. After the initial disappointment I thought, oh well, what's a year if we can still have a baby at the end of it? So I embarked on my course of pills which made me very bloated but, I convinced myself, were definitely worth it.

A year later we were given the all-clear. Still nothing happened. I had the odd mid-cycle spotting of blood and irregualr periods but thought nothing of it, although I had always been like clockwork before. Then one late afternoon on a sunny summer's day I was standing in the kitchen preparing supper when I started to bleed. I went to the lavatory, thinking it was another badly-timed period, but it wouldn't stop. I started to feel a bit frightened and shouted to Johnny to get me a towel. I didn't want to worry him unduly, so I said I was going upstairs to lie down, thinking it would stop. About four towels later I asked him to ring the doctor. I thought I was having a miscarriage. The doctor arrived, examined me and called the hospital to have me admitted. I was given a D and C and sent home the next day, having been told by a sister that Mr X, the gynaecologist who had performed the operation, wanted a word with me and would ring me. I still thought I had had a miscarriage and although I was depressed I felt slightly cheered by the thought that at least I had got pregnant.

A couple of days later I was at home on my own when Mr X rang me. I hadn't been pregnant; I had a large tumour which should be operated on as soon as possible and he suggested I rang my own gynaecologist immediately to arrange a hysterectomy. His words took a moment to sink in; he hadn't actually said the word. 'Are you telling me I have cancer?' I asked in a perfectly normal voice. 'Yes', he replied. 'Thank you so much for letting me know', I said and replaced the receiver. I then sat down on the stool and started to shake. I couldn't stop. I managed to ring Johnny at his office and asked him to come home early as something awful had happened. I was still numb with shock when he arrived hours later – he thought the worst that could have happened was my son being expelled from school, so hadn't hurried! The next week was a nightmare. My gynaecologist was away on holiday so I had to wait. All day and every day I would imagine the cancer like a huge spider spreading inside me. I didn't want to die. I was terrified.

The operation went well, my womb was removed, but I was kindly left with one ovary. I was astounded at what had happened to me as I had always had regular annual smears and it hadn't been that long since I had the laparoscopy – why had nothing been detected? I was told it was a particularly fast-growing form of cancer. I was in hospital for three weeks and during that time my thoughts changed dramatically. I was furious. How dare this happen to me? I refused to admit this was the end of our plans to have a child. It was all quite simple: we would adopt one. I started to ask questions from my hospital bed; I knew that quite a few Irish girls came to have their babies there and I wanted to make enquiries into private adoption. Everyone on the nursing staff treated me very well. I could almost hear them saying, 'just humour her, it's quite natural after what she's been through'. I might as well have been talking to a brick wall.

When I got home things grew worse. I caught a serious bladder infection and was readmitted to hospital for a further week until it cleared up. During this time the seeds of my idea continued to grow but I needed strength to deal with it. It took me a good six months before I was anywhere near back to normal and plucked up courage to discuss adoption with Johnny. He was quite prepared to go along with what I wanted to do, but I got the feeling that he was handing the responsibility over to me in case it shouldn't work out. I was quite happy with that. I have always preferred to get on with things on my own, in my own way, and to present a *fait accompli* at the end. The only thing I insisted on was that we were going to keep the whole operation completely secret – only the children, our solicitor and three friends who would be needed as referees would be allowed to know. My reasons for this were simple; I had a feeling it was going to be difficult (if I'd known just how difficult I don't think I'd have gone on) and if we failed I didn't want sympathy from all our friends, and I also didn't want any negative feelings or opinions from anyone. What people didn't know couldn't be commented on.

I had simply no idea where to start. I only knew there was absolutely no point in trying to adopt in England as we were too old, and anyway there aren't enough babies to go round even for the younger couples. I read an article in a magazine about the plight of babies in South America and an address was given of a woman in Buenos Aires who was helping people. I wrote immediately, sending her our birth certificates and marriage certificate – the originals: I was totally naïve. We never heard from her. Next I tried ringing an old friend of Johnny's who had adopted two boys from Mexico some years ago. I pretended I was asking for a friend of mine. She told me it wasn't worth trying as it was almost impossible now. Another dead end. Another article in another magazine, this time on adoption and fostering and giving the telephone number of the British Agencies for Adoption and Fostering (BAAF). They were extremely unhelpful on anything to do with foreign adoption but did grudgingly suggest I rang an organization called Parent to Parent Information on Adoption Services (PPIAS). I duly rang them and got my first spark of hope. They were very helpful and explained that the first thing I would need for any country would be a social worker's home study. This would have to be done privately as no local authority would want to help. They gave me the telephone number of a private social worker who had done a lot of home studies for people such as ourselves and I got in touch with her immediately. Alison Austin proved to be a real angel. She seemed instinctively to know what we were going through and couldn't have been more helpful.

By now we had decided to try to adopt from Brazil, the most important reason for this being that Johnny was born and brought up there until he came to school in England. It would be wonderful if we could adopt a child who would grow up knowing that he came from the same country where his father was born and thus could maintain connections with his birthplace. Alison thought this an excellent idea and started going through her list of Brazilian adopters. She came across a couple she thought would be happy to share their experiences with us, having adopted a little boy from Recife just a year before. This was our next lucky break. We rang John and Pat Siddons who were absolutely wonderful and told us everything we needed to know – what documents we needed, where to get them translated (Johnny's Portuguese was by now long forgotten) and, most important of all, the woman to contact in Recife who found the babies. She worked alongside a female lawyer who dealt with the legal side of things.

This to us was of paramount importance. In Brazil during recent years there has been an ever-increasing boom in the business of selling babies. These children are not only sold to childless couples for vast sums of money, but also to paedophiles and to unscrupulous clinics for spare parts. There are thirty million unwanted children in Brazil, and for many of them this was their fate. We were determined to do everything legally and above-board; I don't think anyone should buy or sell a human being. Pat Siddons also told us of the pitfalls – Brazilians don't like writing letters, and any letters had to be written in Portuguese. We had to be prepared for a long wait, and patience has never been a virtue of mine. Fortunately we had a big advantage over the Siddons who had to employ translators – Johnny's uncle, who had lived in Brazil nearly all his life, was now living over here. He agreed to write our letters and make the odd telephone call, provided it was on our telephone.

The first letter was the most difficult; I was writing to ask for our child and I had to be fairly specific. We had decided we would prefer a boy – in retrospect this was just as well, as in Brazil it is very difficult to adopt girls, they are kept as money earners: maids are always in demand! We also had to be realistic and honest in saying we did not feel we could take a completely black child as we live in the middle of a field near a small village in Hampshire, and did not feel it would be fair to him to grow up with no other children like him around. If we had lived in London, a multi-cultural society, it would have been different.

We sent photographs of ourselves, the house, the dogs, the room he would have and anything else we could think of. Months went by and we heard nothing, then at last a letter came. I was almost beside myself with excitement, but of course we had to wait until Uncle Jimmy received it for the translation. It was what we wanted to hear. Yes, they could find a little boy for us but it could take some time in view of the fact that we wanted a light-skinned child, as Recife is in the north of Brazil and 90 per cent of the babies born there are very dark. However, they would keep us informed. We were so happy; at last someone had given us hope. Gradually over the months hope diminished; no one contacted us. Poor Pat Siddons must have been so fed up with me, but she was the only person I could call up and moan to, she was so understanding and luckily is a very positive person (as I am normally) and just told me to hang on in there (thanks for keeping me going, Pat). I decided it was a waste of time writing letters and we would have to take out an overdraft for telephone calls. As luck would have it, Uncle Jimmy introduced us to a charming Brazilian friend of his who lives over here as she is married to an Englishman. Believe it or not, she came here from Recife. Ceca Millar became our next invaluable friend. She agreed – to her husband's horror – to make all our telephone calls for us and send us the bill. She was also going home to Recife for the summer and said she would contact Helena, the woman looking for our baby. It was another glimmer of hope to keep us going over the next few months.

I found myself getting more and more obsessed with our unknown Brazilian baby. I couldn't think about anything else, everything seemed so unfair. Each time we made progress it seemed that someone put a banana skin under our feet and we would have to start again. I knew I had to do something to take my mind off what was – or wasn't – happening. I enrolled at a local college to study psychology, something that had always interested me, and, I told myself, if we weren't successful in adopting a child, it was something that I could hopefully use later on. I studied for nearly two years and enjoyed it immensely. I decided I would like to work with children – possibly because I felt I would be too judgmental to work with adults. I went as far as going to talk to the NSPCC locally, as by now I had become fairly philosophical about our adoption and was trying to tell myself that what was meant to be would be – or not. Then out of the blue we got a call from Ceca to tell us of her discussions with Helena in Recife: there was a pregnant woman who was white and healthy, the baby was due at the end of June and if it was a boy he would be ours. I didn't dare get too excited, we had travelled this road before, but somewhere inside of me I felt that maybe this was it. I am very superstitious, and as Ceca's call came through on our birthday in April (Johnny and I share a birthday) I remember thinking that piece of news was the best present we could have.

I was right, but it happened sooner than we thought. At 8.30 a.m. on 22 May, Ceca rang us to say Helena had just telephoned her with the news that we had a little boy who was born at 1 a.m. He was five weeks premature, and what did we want to call him as he must be registered immediately? I was completely stunned. 'Harry' I managed to gulp down the telephone, and said I would ring back later. Johnny was out in the garden. I shot outside and screamed, 'We've got a little boy'. He was very quiet and said, 'Oh, well I think I'll just take the dogs for a walk'. When he returned an hour later he said 'I think we'd better open the pink champagne'. Which is exactly what we did. I thought I was going to burst with excitement; I wanted to shout from the rooftops and tell the world, but of course I couldn't, as no one knew. However, I could tell my daughter Jessica who was at home. I rushed into her bedroom and shouted, 'Wake up, you've got a little brother'. She was over the moon and joined us in the champagne. We also rang my son, Kaj, who was equally thrilled. I must say, during all the traumatic time which we had been through, both the children were a big comfort and supported us completely.

Once the elation and celebration had subsided we were left thinking, 'What now?' After more telephone calls to Brazil we were told that we had to wait until a date could be fixed with a judge to arrange the Brazilian adoption, but this should take only a week or so. I booked our tickets to Recife and we decided that Jessica would come with us to collect her new brother. A week later still no hearing had been arranged. I changed the tickets. More telephone calls. Time was of the utmost importance as all courts go on holiday at the end of June through until September and I knew that a premature baby might not survive three months. I had a vague idea of what his living conditions would be like and it was highly unlikely that a doctor would be called if he fell ill, as no one had any money to pay for him. I rebooked our flights for the following week and the same thing happened again – we were told not to come as the judge was busy. I had reached the end of my tether by now; I had lost a stone in weight, and all I wanted to do was go and collect my baby. The girl in the travel agency was fantastic. I had explained to her why we were such indecisive travellers and she hadn't so much as murmured each time she had to change our tickets. This time I told her to book us definitely on 14 June and there would be no changes. We then asked Ceca to call Brazil again and say that this was when we would arrive, whether or not a court hearing could be arranged.

Next, I rushed off to our nearest town and into a Mothercare shop. Up to now I hadn't bought anything for the baby, it seemed like tempting fate. We had decorated our smallest spare room, but not in anything overtly childish in case anyone should guess what we were up to. The assistant in Mothercare must have thought I was quite mad when I explained that we had just had a new baby who was very small and I hadn't seen him yet. She kept trying to make me buy babygros and vests, and I said he was in Brazil and that all those things were far too hot. All I needed was a moses basket, some nappies and sterilizing equipment. She eventually got the message, and I staggered home under a mound of nappies and baby equipment, having quite forgotten after seventeen years how much they seem to need.

Four days later we were on our way to Paris to catch the Air France plane to Recife. I don't think the realization of what was happening dawned on me until about two in the morning when everyone around me seemed to be asleep, and being six miles high I felt quite in limbo and as though it was someone else going through the whole experience. Suddenly the past two years all seemed like some sort of dream – or nightmare depending on how one looked at it – and now this was reality, a new person was going to join the family. Would I love him immediately? What if he was ugly? I had two very good-looking children; would I be biased? Would I be disappointed in him? Hundreds of questions started entering my mind, questions I had never thought of at all in the past two years, but somehow none of them seemed to require an answer and it seemed that as soon as they entered my mind they only stayed fleetingly and then were gone again. I slept.

We arrived at our hotel in Recife at 2.30 a.m. local time, and, after flying nearly 6,000 miles, we were quite tired and thought we would be able to have a good rest before contacting Helena the following day to arrange to see our baby. It was not to be like that. There was a message waiting for us at the reception desk saying that our court hearing had been fixed for 9 a.m. that day and that we would be collected at 8.15 a.m. The message was from Ceca's sister-in-law Zeze whom we had never met, but she had heard from Ceca what was happening and volunteered to collect us and come to court with us and do our translating. Another guardian angel sent to help us. We were so lucky having these connections, it must be very much harder for those people going to Brazil who know no one.

We were ready and waiting before 8.15. Zeze arrived on time – a very un-Brazilian habit. She explained that the lawyer was also meeting us and then we would all go off to the court. Rita, our lawyer, arrived about 8.45, and we went off in convoy to a little village outside Recife which was just in a different district. The reason for choosing this area was that the judge in the Recife court kept changing, and was also demanding money under the table from foreigners wanting to adopt, and on top of all this there was a very long waiting-list. When we finally arrived at our court I couldn't believe my eyes. It was rather like a scene out of a B movie; everyone was sitting around on the steps or on the floor inside the building and you quite expected chickens to appear to add to the atmosphere of the country court. Someone was waiting for us, a small brown-haired woman who must have once been very beautiful. We were introduced. This was the mother of our son. She had insisted on coming to court and meeting us before the adoption as if she didn't like us she would have said 'No'. How can I explain how I felt? There are no words that can explain my emotions. Here was a woman who through no fault of her own, only through extreme poverty, was being forced to give away her own child and I knew she was only doing it because she truly loved him. It was the biggest gift she could give him. We all held hands and kissed. I couldn't even tell her properly how I felt, I asked Zeze to try and tell her.

Suddenly we were all summoned into a small, very hot and stuffy room where our judge presided. We all sat down. He read through our papers and then through our translator asked, 'Have you seen the baby?' We looked at each other, it seemed incredible. 'No', we replied. 'Aren't you worried about adopting a baby you haven't seen?' Sheer madness, but we weren't. Somehow we just knew he was meant for us. The judge shrugged and we got on with the business at hand. Suddenly he came to something in our papers and stopped. How long had we been married? The answer was five years in ten days' time. He was a judge who did everything by the book. Couples could not adopt unless they had been married for five years to the day. I thought I would die – we couldn't come back in ten days' time as the judge would be on holiday and the court would be closed. We certainly couldn't wait in Recife until September. He relented. He wouldn't sign full adoption papers but he would make us Harry's legal guardians and give permission for a passport to be granted so he could leave the country. In September we would receive his adoption papers and his new birth certificate – in our name. I could have kissed him.

We had another slight hiccup when he was looking at photographs of our house, part of which is six hundred years old, and he was worried in case we had a ghost. We assured him we didn't. We left the court feeling jubilant. Now we could go and collect our son, but first we had to stop at an ice-cream parlour to collect Helena (in whose flat Harry was being kept) as she worked there part-time. I couldn't believe this was real. Eventually we arrived at a small block of flats. We got into the lift and the top button was pressed. My heart was beating so fast I thought I might faint. We went into a large sitting room and could hear the sound of babies crying from somewhere else in the apartment. A maid went padding off and came back a couple of minutes later with a tiny bundle. I shook my head and made a gesture for her to give him to Magda, his natural mother. She held him for a minute and whispered to him, then came across the room and put him in my arms. We all cried. He was so tiny and sweet and I loved him at first sight. We were about to change his whole world and I just wanted him to love us as we loved him. I gave him to Johnny who could hold him in one hand. It was one of the happiest moments of my life. Magda left quietly. I hope she knew what joy she had given us; I think she did.

We took Harry back to the hotel and neither Jessica nor I could take our eyes off him; she adored him too. We had brought milk from England as the Brazilian powdered milk is not very good. He had to be fed every three hours and bathed three times a day to keep him cool.

The latter proved amusing as we bought a baby bath but couldn't fill it from the basin, so Johnny had to stand in the shower with the bath on his head to fill it up. Luckily the hotel had a good snack-bar downstairs where we would eat each evening with Harry in his basket beside us.

The following day we had to go to the Notary to get everything stamped and finalized. From there we had to go to the police station to get Harry his own passport, which proved to be a long process. However, we emerged unscathed and triumphant with the all-important green passport. A couple of days later we made a very important visit to a top paediatrician recommended by Zeze. I didn't think I could have stood it if we had found anything wrong with Harry once we had returned to England. We had him thoroughly examined – under loud protest – and tested for Aids, syphilis and hepatitis. He passed on every test. From there we had to go to the British Embassy. We were shown a somewhat lengthy text and asked to read it. It stated that British subjects wishing to adopt from Brazil had to apply in writing to the Home Office for an entry permit for the child. Did we know this? 'No,' we lied. We also told the gentleman in question that we had never seen the document we had just read. He gave us a knowing look, smiled and explained that it was his job to show it to us. The reason we said what we did was because we already knew the 'catch 22' situation within the Home Office. On applying for an entry permit you are told to go and find your child first, come back and inform the Home Office, who will then deal with it. As there is a four-year pile-up your baby would either be dead or well beyond infancy should you eventually be granted your permit. One just has to trust to luck and the discretion of the immigration officer on entering this country.

In the next couple of days we even managed to do a bit of sight-seeing. We bought Harry some things to take home so that when he is older we can talk about his 'other' country. We had been in Recife for only a week and were extraordinarily lucky to have done everything so quickly – basically all thanks to Zeze. In Brazil it is a case of who you know, not what you know. Johnny had agreed that we could fly home via Rio de Janeiro, as I desperately wanted to see it and he wanted to go back after so many years away. We stayed two days there on Copacabano Beach and took Harry right up to the top of the Corcorada in his basket. I fell in love with the city, it is so exciting and visually stunning.

Then began the journey home. Harry was magic and slept nearly all the way. When we arrived at Heathrow I was distinctly nervous and

Jessica even more so. Johnny as usual was totally calm. I presented our passports to the immigration official and thought we were going to be waved through. 'Whose is this?' he asked, holding the precious green passport. 'Oh, that's just our baby in the basket', I replied airily. We were then led off to a waiting area full of tired-looking Asians. Jessica was getting in a panic. I calmed her down and started to plan what I'd do if Harry was refused entry. I decided I'd fly back to Paris and then get a friend to come across on a boat so that I could smuggle him in. Luckily I didn't need to break the law. After an hour-and-a-half, during which time a translator was found to translate all our Brazilian papers, we were given a three-month visa for Harry and we went home. A real family at last. Now we had to tell everyone what we had been up to. I can honestly say that with one exception all our friends were fantastic and quite a few burst into tears when they heard – tears of happiness, I might add.

We rang the local Social Services who were very understanding. They said we had to sign a letter of intent of adoption and then Harry would be legally protected in this country. They also told us we must have Harry here a year before we could get his British adoption hearing. We would need visits from a social worker for that year. None of this worried us; we had our wonderful little boy and surely the rest would be plain sailing. We took Harry on holiday to Portugal in October, having got a year's extension on his passport thanks to a very important person we had the good fortune to know in the Home Office.

Our first Christmas together was wonderful. Harry's big brother and sister spoilt him dreadfully and enjoyed every minute of it. We applied for an adoption hearing in the local magistrates' court, having been told it would be a lot cheaper to do it ourselves rather than using a solicitor. Jo, the social worker, was sweet and said she didn't foresee any problems. None of us expected that the court would appoint a guardian *ad litem*. Mrs X obviously had reservations about foreign adoption from the start. She was also from an authority which had recently received considerable press and radio publicity over a mixed-race child being taken away from his white foster parents. She was very much against Harry being privately educated. What problems had we considered would effect a black child in a predominantly white school? Would it not be wrong for him to go to private schools when he came from a poor background? I am much more volatile than Johnny. I was furious. This was her first meeting with us and she hadn't even seen Harry, but assumed he was black. Also we adopted Harry when he was four weeks old —surely we were his background, or did she expect us to remind him how lucky he was for the rest of his life? I told her that I didn't think background was genetic, it was environmental. At the end of that meeting Johnny quite rightly told me I must keep calm and keep smiling each time we met, as Harry's future could depend on it. I did as he asked but I found it very difficult. Due to Civil Service strikes and bureaucracy they managed to delay our hearing three times, on one occasion by insisting on another medical report to be done by their appointed doctor at our local hospital. This particular doctor was a further obstacle to be overcome. He didn't approve of inter-country adoption by 'geriatric' parents. More smiling. Hypocrisy was becoming my middle name, but it was worth it.

At 9 a.m. on 2 November we dressed Harry in his best clothes and set off for the court. We were with the magistrates for five minutes and the only problem pronounced by the chairperson was that she would like to keep Harry for herself! Then it was all over. Harry was a little English boy and was finally, utterly and irrevocably our very own.

I have tried to help quite a few people since our own experience – some successfully, which has given me great joy. There has been only one person, a friend with grown-up children, like us wanting to adopt a baby, who has ever asked me, 'Didn't you have any doubts during those two years?' I was sure then that she wouldn't adopt because she had had her doubts. We never had any.

9 Inter-country adoption
In whose best interest?

John Triseliotis

This chapter aims to examine (1) the background to inter-country adoption; (2) some of the main recent studies on the subject; and (3) the arguments for and against inter-country adoption.

BACKGROUND

Inter-country adoptions became prominent after the end of the Second World War and they have been closely associated with wars and destruction. More recently there has been a match between an acute scarcity of white babies free for adoption in developed countries and the extremes of poverty in a number of Third World countries. Inter-country adoptions, as currently practised, pose some of the moral and empirical questions traditionally associated with own-country trans-racial adoptions. At the same time inter-country adoptions give rise to additional issues by being both inter-country and trans-racial in nature. (Within the limited space available here only selected aspects of trans-racial adoptions will be discussed which are relevant to inter-country ones).

As with all other types of adoption, motives to adopt from abroad can vary from the wish to create or enlarge a family whilst at the same time offering a home to a needy child, to altruistic and humanitarian motives to 'rescue' children from suffering. A humanitarian motive, as a response to a child's plight, seemed to predominate in those early inter-country adoptions, but this subsequently changed towards meeting the needs of childless couples. Though much still remains to be learned about what motivates people to adopt, a healthy motive is generally seen to be one that aims to provide a home for a needy child rather than a child for a home.

The history of adoption over centuries has fluctuated between these two opposites. The current expectation, reflected in the British legislation, is that adoption should be practised in the best interests and long-term welfare of the child. In other words, it should be child-centred. Whether this should remain the sole basis for judging own or inter-country adoptions, irrespective of the moral issues involved, is part of the debate. It could be argued that, because of the way they are currently practised, most inter-country adoptions are adult-centred.

For a quarter of a century or so following the end of the Second World War, the image of adoption in Western countries was associated with the provision of healthy white, non-marital infants to healthy, economically and socially sound and largely childless couples. As a result the availability or otherwise of babies for adoption was closely linked to the incidence of non-marital births; to the prevailing attitudes towards such births; and finally to the general social and economic conditions. It is now widely acknowledged that the harsh economic conditions and the stigma which surrounded non-marital births until recently in Western countries were decisive factors behind most relinquishments of children for adoption. In spite of this the demand for healthy infants almost always exceeded the supply. Not surprisingly perhaps, adoption societies generally applied stringent criteria of who could adopt. When the scarcity of babies became acute after the late 1960s because of improved social conditions, and the availability of contraceptive and abortion facilities, many would-be adopters turned their attention mainly to the children of Third World countries.

As now, the demand for babies came from the more prosperous countries, initially the USA. Based on prevailing ideas about matching, the effort at first was to obtain children as near as possible to the characteristics of the adopters. As a result most attention went first to white children from less privileged countries at the time such as Germany, Greece and later Japan. As the supply of white inter-country children also started to dry up, would-be adopters began to compromise on issues concerning the degree of the child's pigmentation, and they turned their attention to other continents such as Asia and Latin America. It was the Korean War, though, which created conditions that signalled one of the largest supplies of children for adoption to developed countries lasting until the early 1980s. One inter-country adoption agency placed over 14,000 Korean children in the USA by 1976 (Holt International Children's Services Inc. Annual Report 1975 and Annual Report 1976 – Eugene Oregon).

WHITE BABY FAMINE

A new and more extensive pattern of inter-country adoptions started in the early 1970s that was to encompass many Third World countries besides Korea, including war-stricken Vietnam. This new wave was only partly related to the war in Vietnam and more to the now acute shortage of babies for adoption in Western countries coinciding with extensive poverty and over-population in Asia and Latin America. As an example of the shortage of white healthy babies in developed countries, in Sweden about 1,000 adoptions per year were registered annually during the early 1950s, whereas during the 1970s they fell to around 100 (Bungerfeldt 1979). In England and Wales adoptions by non-relatives reached a peak of 12,372 in 1968 but fell to about a third of this figure by the late 1980s. In the late 1960s about four out of every five children adopted were less than 12 months old at placement whereas by the late 1980s such children represented only about two in every five. In Holland, own-country adoptions reached a peak of 747 in 1970, but in the following years these gradually disappeared (Hoksbergen 1990).

Western countries responded to this acute shortage of babies for adoption in their own countries in three different ways. At one extreme, among European countries, Scandinavia, Germany, The Netherlands, France and Italy went all out for inter-country adoptions from Third World countries. It is estimated that 6,000 children from such countries had been adopted in Norway by 1987, about 30,000 in Sweden and 20,000 in Holland. In 1984, 94 per cent of all adoptions in Holland were from abroad (Loenen and Hoksbergen 1986, Hoksbergen 1990). Approximately two-thirds of the children coming in were less than a year old and only 16 per cent were more than 3 years old. Adoption, especially in Northern Europe, is now synonymous with inter-country adoption. Pilotti (1985) has drawn attention to the growing proportion of young healthy children included in these figures. Initially a fair proportion of the children were older and some were handicapped, but because of adaptation difficulties posed by the children adopters have more recently turned their attention to young infants who were not usually orphaned or abandoned.

At the other extreme, and unlike the continent of Europe, Britain responded by turning its attention to its own 'special needs' children with apparently very few inter-country adoptions taking place. 'Special needs' was the term used to describe children who fell outside the traditional image of who is an adoptable child. These were children who were older, handicapped, had learning difficulties or were members of a sibling group. The theoretical underpinning for the move to secure permanent families, preferably through adoption, for such children, came from two major sources. First, from the general move towards treating disadvantaged children and adults outside institutions and therefore in the community, with the emphasis on family care. Second, from the optimism conveyed by studies suggesting that, under favourable conditions, children who had experienced separations, deprivations and institutionalization could recover from earlier psychological traumas (e.g. Kadushin 1970, Clarke and Clarke 1976, Tizard 1977, Triseliotis and Russell 1984). Almost all adoption agencies in Britain focused their attention on finding homes for children whose families were unable or unwilling to care for them. Campaigns asking for 'a home for a child' became widespread and featured frequently on television. In contrast, inter-country adoptions rarely featured in the policies and plans of these agencies.

BAAF's booklet on inter-country adoption concluded that no Social Services Department and no voluntary societies had programmes to bring children to the UK for adoption (BAAF 1983). Though inter-country adoptions in Britain may be few compared to some other Western countries, their extent is unknown. In contrast to BAAF's earlier estimations, Margaret Bennett, a London solicitor, in a recent address to the International Bar Association Conference in Strasbourg, claimed that at least 2,000 foreign babies are thought to be brought into Britain each year, including orphans who are bought and sold in Brazil and other Latin American countries (*The Times*, 6 October 1989). A Home Office minister said in a written reply that 149 Romanian children had been allowed to come to Britain to be adopted (*The Times*, 14 February 1991). Perhaps the most that can be said is that there is no explicit British policy with regard to inter-country adoptions, though a blind eye might be turned as long as the practice did not assume large proportions.

The airlift to Britain of Vietnamese children in 1975 was possibly the only organized inter-country adoption effort in Britain. The low profile kept by inter-country adoptions in Britain should be viewed in the light of the virtual embargo on own-country trans-racial placements by the early 1980s. The halt to such placements, both in Britain and the USA, was attributed to serious doubts about its effect on the children and to organized resistance by sections of the black community and particularly on the part of both black and white social workers. There is a big difference, of course, between preventing trans-racial placements through finding suitable in-race ones, and removing happily settled children from trans-racial homes.

In contrast to the above patterns of inter-country adoption the USA has followed a middle way. Attention to 'special needs' children there seems to have gone hand-in-hand with inter-country adoptions, although the excess of inter-country over own-country adoptions never reached the level observed in some Continental countries. In a spirited defence of inter-country adoptions Joe (1978) claimed that between 1968 and 1975 foreign adoptions in the USA more than tripled, from 1,612 to 5,633 annually. Pilotti (1985) quotes figures demonstrating that from the mid-1970s Latin America became the main source of supply for inter-country adoptions in the States.

The demand for babies has fostered a back-street trafficking in children and has also led to the kidnapping and sale of children. Because of the demand, profit-making agencies have been set up in some countries whose sole aim is to traffic in Third World children. A black market in kidnapped babies, particularly from Latin America, is being fuelled by demand from couples in North America and Western Europe. Many couples do not even realize that they have adopted kidnapped children. It is estimated that in Brazil alone 16,000 babies disappear each year. The problem is so serious that genetic fingerprinting, which is claimed as a conclusive test of parentage, is being suggested as a measure to be used in English courts for immigration purposes to identify kidnapped babies. (See Margaret Bennett's talk to the International Bar Association reported in the *Daily Telegraph* on 29 September 1988.) Not infrequently, adoptions take place by proxy through third parties with little or no control over the suitability of the adopters.

Many of the supporters of inter-country adoptions would favour the setting-up and accreditation of adoption agencies in both recipient and donor countries to supervise the arrangements. A particular need is to ensure that the parents, where they exist, can be found to consent to relinquishing the child, and that the adopters have been properly assessed as suitable. Such agencies operate in some countries as a form of self-regulation, but they usually co-exist with the illegal trafficking. Attention would also need to be paid to the training and preparation of couples to become inter-country adopters. At present the laws of most donor and recipient countries are so loose and imprecise that almost anything can be arranged and made to look legal. (At the time of writing, adoption procedures in the UK are currently under review and a discussion paper on inter-country adoption is expected in the summer of 1991.)

RECENT STUDIES

Outcome studies involving children are generally fraught with methodological difficulties, and adoption is no exception. Some of the difficulties have to do with establishing baselines, identifying outcome criteria and developing suitable measuring tools. In this type of adoption, who sets the criteria and who carries out the research is a further bone of contention. (For example, some of the Swedish studies have been carried out under the aegis of organizations sponsoring inter-country adoptions.) Furthermore, the use of contrast or control groups is not often possible. Comparing studies is also made difficult because they took place at different points following the child's arrival or placement in its new country, with different objectives in mind and using different methodological approaches. Most studies have concentrated on the first few years following arrival or up to adolescence, but there is only one study, as far as it could be established, which has followed adoptees into their late teens and none that went beyond. Most studies have relied on parents' and teachers' reports and only a few have interviewed adoptees.

As with own-country trans-racial adoptions, studies of inter-country adoption have focused on two main issues: first, how children are functioning within the family, school, etc.; and secondly, those concerned with racial and ethnic identification. The way most studies separate 'adjustment' within the family, school, etc. from issues of 'racial and ethnic identity' may be viewed as artificial, because behaviour which is described as 'maladjusted' may have its origins in feelings and reactions concerned with 'racial and ethnic identity' unless the latter concept is too narrowly defined. Interestingly, McRoy and Zurcher (1983) found no relationship between measures of racial identification and self-esteem, but further study is needed.

The children's functioning and adjustment

There are many similarities between the outcomes of own-country trans-racially-placed children and those of inter-country adoption. All studies carried out in the immediate years following arrival and adoptive placement suggest that on the whole the children quickly overcome developmental, linguistic and behavioural difficulties. According to the studies, the children's general adjustment does not seem to differ much from own-country trans-racially or intra-racially-placed children and in some instances it is even better. More persistent problems appear to be related to older age on arrival. This may also signify earlier distressing experiences in the country of origin, but for obvious reasons this aspect is not well documented by the studies.

Simon and Alstein (1987), who carried out studies in trans-racial adoptions including some inter-country ones from the 1970s onwards, comment that trans-racial adoptions in the USA 'were not halted because data indicated that it was a failure and/or that their adoptive families suffered any damaging social or psychological effect'. It was not stopped, they go on to claim, 'because transracial adoptees were expressing racial confusion or negative self-image . . . but because child welfare agencies no longer saw it as politically expedient' (Simon and Alstein 1987: 141). Gill and Jackson (1983), on the basis of their study of trans-racial adoption in Britain, reported that in terms of family functioning and the level of integration into family, performance in school both academically and socially, and general 'adjustment', the children were average or above average in their responses and appeared to have suffered no harm. These studies have followed the children through to adolescence and the results continued to reflect this apparently positive picture.

Feigelman and Silverman (1984), relying on the perceptions of adoptive parents, contrasted the long-term adjustments of Colombian, Korean and Afro-American trans-racial adoptees with those of own-racially adopted whites. After adoptees had been in their adoptive homes for at least six years, the results showed that the adolescent and school-aged inter-country adoptees were no more poorly adjusted than their intra-racially adopted counterparts. In fact, Korean adoptees were better adjusted than white adolescents. It was only with regard to their appearance that Koreans showed more of a negative response than white adolescent adoptees. Koreans, though older on adoption (mean age 5.3 years), recorded better achievements than the whites (mean age 3.2 years). Some signs of poorer adjustment as compared with their white counterparts are explained by the older ages at placement of the inter-country adoptees. (It is fair to add that by the follow-up stage the data were based on only 372, or 34 per cent, of responses compared to an initial sample population of 1,100.)

Kim (1978) also concluded from a postal questionnaire, which relied on parental response, that adopted Korean children progressed very well in all areas of their lives and indicated no special problems of overall long-term adjustment. Their self-concept was 'remarkably similar' to that of other American teenagers. A slightly different picture is conveyed by Rathburn (1965), who in a small study of thirty-eight children from different countries adopted in the USA, found that some time after placement about one-fifth of the children were displaying serious behavioural problems. Five years later, when the children were aged between 6 and 16 years of age, contact was established with all but five of them. At this stage almost a third were thought to have adjustment problems, with two children regarded as clinically distressed and in need of therapy. It is not clear how far such problems were related to their adoption or to other factors.

Cederblad (1982) summarized a number of Scandinavian studies of inter-country adoption which mostly confirmed the findings of the American ones. She quotes a study by Pruzan (1977) of 168 children who had been in Denmark for at least two years and who were aged between 8 and 12 years old at interview. They were found to be as well adjusted as a similar group of Danish-born children. Contrary to other studies that refer to the linguistic difficulties experienced by older children, this one claims that the children had adjusted well at school and that specific educational disabilities were no more prevalent among them than among the Danish reference children. Gardell (1979) studied 207 youngsters aged 10 to 18 years old at a time when they had been with their adoptive families for at least four years, and about 70 per cent had been living in Sweden for over nine years. He found that only 4 per cent of the children who were aged less than 18 months on arrival, as compared to 64 per cent of those who were 6 years or older, had 'serious adjustment problems'. At the time of the follow-up study a quarter of all the families reported that the children displayed problems 'not usually experienced in families with children of the same age'. The exact nature of these problems is not recorded, nor are they broken down by age on arrival.

Gunnarby *et al.* (1982) in a study of 146 children in Uppsala, most of whom had been in Sweden for periods of one to five years, found that from a third to two-fifths had initial problems of adjustment, including poor appetite and sleep, separation anxiety, temper outbursts and aggression, but that most of these problems gradually disappeared. However, those children who were aged from 4 to 7 years old on arrival in Sweden had more persistent problems than those arriving earlier. Similarly, Hofvander *et al.* (1978), in a preliminary study of 52 children, found that those who went to Sweden before they were a year old had adjusted positively and developed normal language skills. Those who were older on arrival passed through a more complicated and protracted adjustment process. In a few children, the problems persisted after the two-year period following arrival. Perhaps as a result of such experiences, in recent years there has been a pronounced switch in all countries towards the adoption of much younger children.

The Swedish studies quoted and a Dutch study (Loenen and Hoksbergen 1986) referred to linguistic difficulties and problems of physical health and adjustment during the earlier stages, but these diminished or disappeared by the follow-up stages. In a more recent paper, Hoksbergen (1990) found that 5.7 per cent of all inter-country adopted children needed residential care at some time, which was three times more than in the case of own-country children. He also found that the older the child at placement, the greater the risk of obtaining high scores on 'delinquent and uncommunicative syndromes' in boys, and on 'cruel, depressed and schizoid syndromes' in girls. Later on he adds that 'because of problems with adoptive children, adopting an older child has become less and less popular in Holland' (p. 19). The only British study on inter-country adoptions known to the writer is by Ahlijah (1990). The author sent a postal questionnaire to sixty families who had adopted from abroad, and forty-six were returned. Ahlijah acknowledges the possible bias of her sample as the names were provided by two pressure groups, PPIAS and STORK. About three-quarters of the adopters were childless, so the altruistic motive may be less prevalent here, and over 80 per cent belonged to the professional classes. Ahlijah speculates that 'a substantial number of couples adopted from abroad because they could not adopt at home' (Ahlijah 1990: 58). Most of those adopting were in their thirties, which is not far out for in-country baby adoption. Almost three-quarters of the children were below the age of 2 years old at the time of placement. With the exception of two African children and one West Indian child, the rest were almost equally divided between Asian countries and Latin America. Seven of the couples in the study indicated that because of their child they consciously made a decision to live in areas with a higher population mix. The participants in the study expressed considerable satisfaction with the way adoption was working for them and with the children's adjustment. Reflecting on this, the author acknowledges the possibility 'that only families who have good adoptions have maintained contact with PPIAS and STORK and have responded to the questionnaire' (ibid: 59).

Racial and ethnic identification

Almost all the studies quoted earlier which reported good family and school 'adjustments' also suggested certain concerns about the children's racial and ethnic identification. Again, these referred to own-country trans-racial as well as inter-country adoptions. For example, Gill and Jackson (1983) acknowledged that the evidence paints a picture of children who, although not directly denying their racial background, perceived themselves to be 'white' in all but skin colour (Gill and Jackson 1983: 18). They go on to explain the lack of racial identity within the children by relating it in particular to class changes which remove them from contact with black people; to the lack of emphasis parents give to racial issues; and the unease they felt about the tension between integration and differentiation. 'All the children's coping mechanisms were based on denying their racial background' (ibid: 137). These comments prompted Small (1986) to express puzzlement as to why the researchers then appear to minimize the problems of identity confusion. Support for his comments would come from Johnson *et al*. (1987) when they concluded from their recent study that the trans-racially-placed child's sense of racial identity stops growing, while that of the black child in a black family does not and therefore overtakes that of the former child. Simon and Alstein (1987) play down broadly similar findings from their studies. For example, 60 per cent of the study sample expressed a preference for dating white people and a third of those interviewed did not describe themselves as black. McRoy and Zurcher (1983) suggest that the most 'whole' personalities were those who attended racially-integrated schools and whose families resided in a racially-integrated community. Fanshel (1972), in one of the earliest studies which looked at how trans-racially-placed American Indian children were faring when still under the age of 5 years, concluded that the children were, by and large, 'very secure and obviously feeling loved and wanted in their adoptive homes' (Fanshel 1972: 339). Commenting on the moral dilemmas raised by such adoptions, he leaves it to the Indian people to determine whether their children can be placed in white homes. The adoption of Indian American children by white families came to a halt in the 1970s.

Kim (1976) and Feigelman and Silverman (1984) noted the discomfort expressed by Korean adolescents adopted in the USA about their appearance, though this was only one of the few areas where adopted Korean youths were likely to have problems. According to Kim, only a very small proportion (8 per cent) of Korean adolescents identified themselves as 'Koreans'. As mentioned earlier, there is a dearth of studies exploring the views, attitudes and perceptions of inter-country adopted teenagers and adults. Possibly the only one available is by Dalen and Saetersdal (1987), who carried out intensive interviews with forty-one adopted teenagers and young adults (mainly from Vietnam) and with their parents. They found that whereas most of the adoptees adjusted well both psychologically and socially during childhood, as they reached adulthood they felt themselves driven into a more 'marginal position', as they had to face more direct situations of discrimination. The authors add:

> in many respects it is fair to say that they live in a psychological no man's land because they at the same time both belong and do not belong. Their position is marginal. Their behaviour indicates that they must fight to be recognised as fully accepted citizens though they avoid contact with unknown people and with situations where they might be rejected, discriminated or subjected to embarrassing positive behaviour. They try to surround themselves with secure friends.
>
> (Dalen and Saetersdal 1987: 43)

One adoptee is quoted as saying,

> I did not dare go in there and pay for petrol. I do not know why. I was afraid. It was perhaps that deep inside I felt that they knew I was different. It was usually when I was alone that people have been making nasty comments.
>
> (ibid: 44)

THE ARGUMENTS FOR AND AGAINST INTER-COUNTRY ADOPTIONS

The arguments for or against inter-country adoptions have similarities to and some differences from own-country trans-racial placements. Indeed, questions have always been asked about the legitimacy of adoption as practised in Western countries. Most questions still have to do with how free relinquishing parents really are when giving up a child for adoption. Economic and social constraints and pressures are said to be often responsible for relinquishment decisions. Other questions have to do with whether adoption is in the best interests of the child. Not surprisingly, perhaps, similar questions are now being asked about inter-country adoptions.

It is arguable whether there is such a thing as an absolutely free choice, and what we may be talking about is relative freedom from pressures for parents who relinquish children. Pressures operating on relinquishing parents which limit choice can include the absence or insufficiency of practical resources, undue pressures from relatives, possible career considerations, and finally internal pressures relating to the state of a parent's mental or emotional state and parental perceptions about their ability to parent a child. Although it would be nice to think that no parent should feel pressurized, for whatever reason, to relinquish a child, the fact remains that such pressures have featured in many own-country adoptions over the years and are presently featuring in most inter-country adoptions. No doubt the easier availability of contraceptive facilities and of abortion have contributed to the dramatic reduction, but the main reasons for this have been the lessening of stigma and improved economic and social conditions in Western countries. The same would become the case if improved social and economic conditions were to be attained in Third World countries. Retrospective studies of mothers who relinquished children of their own nationality fifteen to thirty years ago claim that most of them felt under extreme pressure, and that relinquishment was frequently not based on free choice (Pannor *et al.* 1978; Winkler and Keppel 1984; Bouchier and Lambert 1990). Many of these mothers have been reported as continuing to carry the long-term adverse effects of their loss. To ameliorate this, an increasing number of agencies are now moving towards more 'open' forms of adoption, with contact preserved.

The element of free choice can also be taken away by the State, under certain circumstances, such as through freeing for adoption or by the court dispensing with parental consent. As to whether adoption is in the best interests of the child, studies generally suggest that the psychological parenting of a child by people who are not his parents can work almost as well as own-parent rearing (Raynor 1980; Bohman 1970; Seglow *et al.* 1972; Lambert and Streather 1980; Triseliotis and Russell 1984).

ECUMENICAL HUMANITARIANISM OR EXPLOITATION?

The moral arguments advanced in favour of inter-country adoption do not differ much from those put forward in support of adoption in general. A widespread view is that rapid communication systems have reduced the whole world to one community. Common humanity and collective responsibility towards each other can no longer be confined within national boundaries. Charity, if that's what adoption is about, does not stop at home or at state frontiers. Children suffering from the devastation of wars, famines, dispersions, abandonment or orphanhood are the concern of everybody and especially when their own families or countries cannot care for them. Plant (1990) argues that with jet liners and instant communications the world has become a global village, and as a result it would be anachronistic 'in matters of duty and charity, to attach great significance to local or national boundaries'. Further on he argues that 'to limit my moral responsibility I should not read or watch television reports of drought and disaster. I should not look at charity advertisements'.

Although the proponents of inter-country adoption would recognize that adoption can touch only a fraction of the magnitude of need present in the supply countries, they would view it as grossly immoral to stand by when there are families willing to offer the children a new home with good prospects in another country. After all, it could be further argued, when adoption legislation was introduced in Britain in the 1920s it was also against a background of a recent war and of considerable poverty and deprivation, with relinquishing parents having possibly as little choice as relinquishing parents in Third World countries have now. To wait for improved social conditions before acting to give parents and countries a real choice would be tantamount to sacrificing an existing generation of children who need new families now. The alternative to adoption, for many children, could be death through illness and malnutrition, or rearing in orphanages with their high death rates and generally negative outcomes.

The moral arguments for the opponents of inter-country adoption, including UN organizations, could be summarized as follows. In a truly ecumenical society of brotherhood and equality, free of power influences and with no racism, inter-country adoptions would pose no problems. However, we do not live in such a society. The races do not mix freely, racism is widespread, and there is no genuine equality of power between rich and poor nations or white and black people. Whilst the world is getting smaller, nations wish to assert their identities more and emphasize their national boundaries, their customs, religions, dialects and tribal allegiances. What they are asking for is distinctiveness, not sameness. In addition, the ecumenical altruism claimed on behalf of inter-country adoptions represents the continued exploitation of the poorer by the richer nations, the dictation of the more powerful to the weaker. Most inter-country adoptions have come about not because of humanitarian motives, but mainly because of the acute shortage of white children for adopting in developed countries. The main motive is the provision of children to mostly childless, wealthy couples in the West. Far from being a shared activity, inter-country adoptions move in a single direction from Third World to developed countries and they epitomize the exercise of influence and control by the more powerful nations who are seen as 'robbing' Third World countries of their children whilst confirming their inferiority and inadequacy, thus politicizing the whole issue. Kim

(1978), writing about Korean children, remarked that 'although the rescue fantasy seems to have lost its momentum, the whole cause of raising other people's children seems to embrace a new element of self-righteousness, if not outright selfishness'.

The second main argument against inter-country adoptions is that they are largely irrelevant to the needs of Third World children and only help to divert attention from their real needs. Ngabonziza (1988) argues that the legal adoption of a few children overseas, with perhaps the consent of donor and host governments, disguises the needs of millions of children who are left to grow up in poverty or die of disease. Instead, Western governments and adoption workers everywhere should be raising their voices for health and welfare programmes for all children through overseas aid. Following the recent rush to adopt Romanian 'orphans', the Romanian Red Cross is reported to have urged people in the West to spend money to help the authorities there give the children a better life in their own country (*Observer*, 7 January 1990). In the same article it was reported that Social Service departments of British local authorities said they would not consider the processing of applications for inter-country adoptions a 'priority'. Their principal concern was to find adoptive parents for thousands of 'special needs' children currently in local authority care. Is this a chauvinistic or a realistic response in the face of the controversies surrounding trans-racial and inter-country adoptions?

Individuals motivated to help Thirld World children, it is argued, could do so not by uprooting them from their families and countries but by 'adopting' them from a distance instead. A move in this direction would be in line with, though very different from, the new type of adoption which is beginning to emerge in developed countries. As already indicated, adoption is now becoming more 'open', with natural parents having a say in the choice of adopters. Where older children are concerned, the maintenance of links between natural parents and child are increasingly being preserved after adoption. Adoption in the 1990s is likely to become more of a shared activity between genetic and adopting parents, though adopters and children need to have the legal security that goes with adoption. On the negative side, as own-country adoption becomes more open, more couples may of course turn to inter-country adoption in the expectation that they will not have to concern themselves too much with issues about parental access and possible interference. In this respect adopting a child from abroad could almost be viewed as a retrograde step.

A COMMON HUMAN IDENTITY?

The arguments put forward to support inter-country adoption as part of 'ecumenical humanitarianism' could also be expanded to accommodate the concept of a 'common human identity', irrespective of racial, ethnic or cultural background. It could be claimed that paramount in the development of personality is the quality of care that a child receives, whether from actual or from surrogate parents. Leaving aside genetic factors, studies tend to suggest that though issues of origins and personal and social identity for own-race and own-country adoptions are very important, a crucial factor in human development is the quality of care experienced in childhood (Jaffee and Fanshel 1970; Triseliotis and Russell 1984). This would imply that the child's basic need for security, trust and a sense of belonging can be provided by caring psychological parents (Pringle 1980). Though still adhering to the principle of 'a common human identity', some supporters of inter-country adoption, like own-race adoption, would add that issues about the child's sense of racial and cultural identity could be tackled through deliberate efforts on the parents' part.

However, Jones and Else (1977) dismiss the idea of a common human identity, as this amounts to denial of differences and a colour-blind approach. The parents may not judge people by the colour of their skin, but others do. Furthermore, as they add, the socialization of a minority child is complex because the child must be able to live and operate effectively in both the minority and the majority community. Later on they add that if the parents are committed to 'a socialisation into a minority ideology and culture', they have to make a number of deliberate choices. These include the kind of neighbourhood they live in and the social institutions they choose to join and which will determine, to a large degree, the friendships and experiences the family develops; involving themselves in clubs and organizations set up by minority persons; attending cultural events, dealing with minority experiences; joining religious and recreational institutions that have a significant minority membership; sending the children to schools with a significant minority population; and having minority persons as friends.

The observation made earlier that awareness of origins is an important but not the paramount factor in personality development may be true of white children adopted by white families, but it still has to be shown that it also holds true of inter-country or trans-racial adoptions. The argument would be that because of racism and negative discrimination towards black people, issues of racial and ethnic identity may be of as much importance as the quality of care. Small (1986) argues that living in a society that is basically racist exposes those who are confused about their racial identity to pressures, conflicts and suffering not understood by many white people. He is critical of those, including researchers, who fail to recognize 'the identity needs of black children in a racist society' (Small 1986: 81).

Like own-country adoptees, children adopted from abroad have eventually to base their emerging personalities on two sets of parents, one biological and one psychological. They also have to come to terms with the element of loss and 'rejection' by the original family which is implied in all adoptions (Triseliotis 1973). The child who is adopted from abroad may also experience feelings of loss and 'rejection' not only by its parents but also by its own country, though the latter still remains to be substantiated. We know from studies that own-race and own-country adoptees try to find answers to the question of 'who am I?' through knowledge about their antecedents and heritage. Inter-country adopted people should also be able to do so, but because of the way many such adoptions are arranged this is often impossible.

Inter-country adopted children and adults who look different in a predominantly white society are also likely to face hostility and dis-crimination which can undermine their self-esteem and mental health. Ngabonziza (1988), for example, referred to a recent Swiss television programme where adopted youngsters from Korea, India, Lebanon and Zaire all reported that they were suffering from negative racial discrimination. The writer goes on to ask 'whether the child could not be better off in a poorer but more accepting environment in its own country' (Ngabonziza 1988: 39). To what degree the care and love of their adoptive parents is enough to help them withstand this pressure is still uncertain. This may not be different, of course, from the racism experienced by black children reared by their own or other black families, and no parent, irrespective of colour, can control this. Black writers would respond, though, by saying that the black child reared within its own race can develop 'coping mechanisms' to withstand racist pressures. Such mechanisms span the black community's economic life, education and social relationships, and it is these which provide the cultural and psychological framework that gives energy and support to black children – and by extension to inter-country children who are mostly black in a generic sense (see Small 1986: 85–6). However, the precise nature of such mechanisms has yet to be elucidated.

CONCLUSION

Available empirical evidence suggests that inter-country adoptions work as well as own-country placements, but concerns are expressed about the children's lack of racial and ethnic identity and about their exposure to racist behaviour as they grow older. The latter is likely to be experienced as more rejecting and oppressive in countries with very small black populations. Racial identity is more likely to develop when the children live in racially-integrated areas, attend integrated schools and have adopters who acknowledge their racial and ethnic identity.

Whatever the research evidence about the outcome of inter-country adoptions, it cannot sidestep all the moral arguments. The UN looks upon inter-country adoptions as a last resort in providing a child with a family. In its Declaration of Social and Legal Principles relating to the Protection and Welfare of Children, with special reference to Foster Placement and Adoption Nationally and Internationally (1978), part of the UN article 17 states:

> If a child cannot be placed in a foster or adoptive family or cannot in any suitable manner be cared for in the country of origin, inter-country adoption may be considered as an alternative means of providing the child with a family.

REFERENCES

Ahlijah, F. (1990) 'Intercountry Adoption: In Whose Interest?', dissertation submitted for the degree of MSc in Applied Social Studies, Oxford University.

Bohman, M. (1970) *Adopted Children and Their Families*, Stockholm: Proprius.

Bouchier, P. and Lambert, L. (1990) 'Birth mothers and adoption in Scotland', Edinburgh: Report to Family Care.

British Agencies for Adoption and Fostering (1983) *Inter-country Adoptions*, London: BAAF (Second Printing).

Bungerfeldt, G. (1979) *Dèscueso de presentacion del Centro de Adoption con Motivo del Primer Semonario National Sobre Adoption en el Ecuador*, Stockholm: Adoption Centre, pp. 6–7.

Cederblad, M. (1982) *Children Adopted from Abroad and Coming to Sweden after Age Three*, The Swedish National Board for Inter-country Adoption.

Clarke, A. D. B. and Clarke, A. M. (1976) *Early Experience: Myth and Evidence*, London: Open Books.

Dalen, M. and Saetersdal, B. (1987) 'Transracial adoption in Norway', *Adoption and Fostering* 11 (4): 41–6.

Fanshel, D. (1972) *Far From the Reservation*, New York: Columbia University Press.

Feigelman, W. and Silverman, A. R. (1984) 'The long-term effects of transracial adoption', *Social Service Review* 58: 588–662.

Gardell, I. (1979) *Internationelle Adoptioner*, En rapport frän Allmänna Barnhuset, Stockholm: Allmänna Barnhuset.

Gill, O. and Jackson, B. (1983) *Adoption and Race*, London: Batsford.

Gunnarby, A., Hofvander, Y., Sjölin, S. and Sundelin, C. (1982) 'Utländska adoptivbarns hälsotillständ och anpassning till svenska förhällanden', *Läkartidningen* 79 (17): 1697–1705.

Hofvander, Y., Bengstsson, E., Gunnarby, A., Cederblad, M., Kats, M. and Strömholm, S. (1978) 'U-landsadotivbarn-hälsa och anpassning', *Läkartidningen* 75: 4673–80.

Hoksbergen, R. (1990) 'Inter-country adoptions coming of age in Holland', privately circulated paper.

Jaffee, B. and Fanshel, D. (1970) *How They Fared in Adoption*, New York: Columbia University Press.

Joe, B. (1978) 'In defense of inter-country adoption', *Social Service Review* 52: 2–20.

Johnson, R. P., Shireman, J. F. and Watson, K. W. (1987) 'Transracial adoption and the development of black identity at age eight', *Child Welfare* 66: 45–56.

Jones, C. E. and Else, J. F. (1977) 'Racial and cultural issues in adoption', *Child Welfare* 58: 373–82.

Kadushin, A. (1970) *Adopting Older Children*, New York: Columbia University Press.

Kim, D. S. (1976) *Inter-country Adoptions: a study of Self Concept of Adolescent Korean Children who were Adopted by American Families* (PhD dissertation), School of Social Work, University of Glasgow.

—— (1978) 'Issues in transracial adoption and transcultural adoption', *Social Casework* 477–86.

Lambert, L. and Streather, J. (1980) *Children in Changing Families*, London: Macmillan.

Loenen, A. and Hoksbergen, R. (1986) 'Inter-country adoption', *Adoption and Fostering* 10 (2): 22–6.

McRoy, R. and Zurcher, L. (1983) *Transracial and Inracial Adoptees*, Springfield, Ill.: Thomas.

Ngabonziza, D. (1988) 'Inter-country adoption; in whose best interest?', *Adoption and Fostering* 12 (1): 35–46.

Pannor, R., Baran, A. and Sorosky, A. D. (1978) 'Birth parents who relinquished babies for adoption revisited', *Family Process* 17: 329–37.

Pilotti, J. F. (1985) 'Inter-country adoption: a view from Latin America', *Child Welfare* 64 (1): 25–35.

Plant, R. (1990) 'No man is an island – except in ignorance', *The Times*, 1 January 1990: 10.

Pringle, M. L. K. (1980) *The Needs of Children* (second edition), London: Hutchinson.

Pruzan, V. (1977) 'Født i udlandet-adopteret i Danmark', Köpenham, Social forsknings institutet 77.

Rathburn, C. (1965) 'Later adjustment of children following radical separation from family and culture', *American Journal of Orthopsychiatry* 35: 327–35.

Raynor, L. (1980) *The Adopted Child Comes of Age*, London: Allen & Unwin.

Seglow, J., Pringle, M. L. K. and Wedge, P. (1972) *Growing up Adopted*, Windsor: National Foundation for Educational Research.

Simon, R. J. and Alstein, H. (1987) *Transracial Adoptees and their Families*, New York: Praeger.

Small, J. (1986) 'Transracial placements: conflicts and contradictions', in Ahmed, S., Cheetham, J. and Small, J. (eds) *Social Work with Black Children and Their Families*, London: Batsford.

Tizard, B. (1977) *Adoption: A Second Chance*, London: Open Books.

Triseliotis, J. (1973) *In Search of Origins: The Experiences of Adopted People*, London: Routledge & Kegan Paul.

—— (1989) 'Some moral and practical issues in adoption work', *Adoption and Fostering* 13 (2): 21–6.

Triseliotis, J. and Russell, J. (1984) *Hard to Place: The Outcome of Adoption and Residential Care*, London: Heinemann/Gower.

Winkler, R. and Keppel, M. (1984) *Relinquishing Mothers in Adoption: Their Long-Term Adjustment*, Melbourne: Institute of Family Studies, Monograph, No. 3.

Note For information on the Swedish studies, I am indebted to Dr Marianne Cederblad's monograph referred to above.

10 Inter-country adoption

A view from the House of Commons

Peter Thurnham, MP

Over the last few months, I have been in contact with a number of people who are trying to adopt a child from abroad. As an adoptive father myself, I fully know what a complicated business it is. My wife and I, who have four other children, adopted Stephen nearly seven years ago. He originally came from Wales, which I suppose might count as inter-country! Stephen is multiply handicapped and therefore has his own particular needs, but we hope that we have been able to give him the happy and loving home that he deserves. He has recently celebrated his 16th birthday.

Naturally, adopting anybody else's child, especially one with particular handicaps, whether physical or emotional, is an enormous responsibility. When adopting a child from abroad, one is faced with other complicating factors. Inevitably, the burden of responsibility lies heavily with the receiving country. In Britain, that responsibility is taken very seriously by our authorities who believe, in accordance with the principles of the United Nations, that the regulations governing inter-country adoption should be at least as stringent as those operating within the adoptive parents' own country. Consequently, the process can be frustrating, lengthy and often extremely expensive. While the general public expects our authorities to act prudently, many people have expressed their exasperation with a system which appears to rate a doctrine of 'safeguards' higher than a doctrine of compassion. As a result, an alarming degree of hostility seems to have grown up between the decision-makers and their 'clients'. This situation is dangerous and intolerable, since serious delays can lead to profound frustration on the part of prospective adopters, who may then attempt to circumvent the necessary procedures.

My principal experience of inter-country adoption has been in the present context of the Romanian crisis. After Ceausescu's execution, the horrors of his regime were uncovered. Mothers had been forced to have five children. No contraceptives were available. No abortion was allowed. The results of such measures are now well known to us all since the media have uncovered the pathetic, indeed horrific conditions in the orphanages there. The response in Britain was marvellous. Within weeks, well over a dozen organizations were set up to co-ordinate aid and send medical teams out to Romania. The EC Commission recently set up a programme of aid specifically for children in Romania and a total of several million pounds has already been allocated. The media launched various successful campaigns; Blue Peter alone raised over £5 million. Every local newspaper carried its own story of the public-spirited efforts of its community, whether it was transporting medical supplies, clothes and toys in person to the orphanages, or raising the funds to do so.

Clearly, everyone wanted to assist the Romanian authorities in every way possible, and the common humanitarian instinct to help led many people to offer to adopt some of these children. The media have followed these attempts with interest and vividly described some of the difficulties encountered. Typical stories have focused on the terrible confusion and delays, the reams of red tape and bureaucratic obstruction. British couples complained that while their American, German and French counterparts flew home without delay to sympathetic immigration officials, they themselves waited at home, hoping and praying that their child wouldn't have contracted hepatitis B or other even more lethal diseases in the meantime and have died during the coldest winter months. One couple described how their Romanian lawyer would not deal with any more British couples because 'you are treated as though you are criminals for wanting to give a home to these babies'.

The emotive nature of some of this reporting has angered the Social Services, the Home Office and particularly the Department of Health. As the Minister of Health, Virginia Bottomley, warned the House of Commons on 29 October 1990, 'If a child is placed with far from satisfactory adoptive parents, that is described as negligence on the part of the local authority in fulfilling its duties. Difficult judgements must be made, together with checks on criminal and health records, but they are essential in safeguarding a child's welfare.'

It is absolutely right that great care should be taken to protect children from falling into the hands of undesirable parents. The fact that many children are born naturally to unsuitable parents does not in any way diminish the obligation to assess adoptive parents with rigour. Thoroughness is a catchword for child welfare organizations, since they are particularly anxious that certain decisions do not in time prove to be disastrous.

Such anxiety stems, in part, from the recognition that certain policy decisions have in retrospect turned out to be gross errors of judgment. The consequences can be devastating, as was explained to me by Margaret Humphreys of the Child Migrants Trust, which she set up in 1987. Since then she has helped many adults who were transported to former British colonies, some as recently as the 1960s, by child-care charities such as Barnardos, the Church of England Children's Society and the National Children's Home. The majority were sent to Australia – to what was believed to be a better life. Many of these so-called 'orphans', though a great many were not, are now desperate to trace their natural family. This has proved to be an immensely difficult task since vital information relating to their background was either not recorded or was withheld or lost by the charities concerned. Moreover, in the case of the child migrants, it appears that little effort had been made to check the suitability of those who were given care of these children, since they were rarely placed for adoption but instead apprenticed as farm labourers and domestic servants or confined to institutions.

These unhappy chronicles inevitably send a shiver of fear down the backs of the child welfare professions and emphasize the extent of their burden of responsibility. Fortunately, the decisions that surrounded the placement of these children differ markedly from current practice. Perhaps too we have allowed ourselves to become obsessed with the possibility of failure and with the problems related to illegal immigration and baby trafficking. Clearly, these fears will remain genuine unless and until the international community demonstrates the political will to act efficiently and co-operatively.

Our Government is currently reviewing the whole of the adoption legislation, and the Department of Health will shortly be issuing a working paper specifically on procedures for inter-country adoption. I know that Virginia Bottomley is anxious that the regulations be made more efficient, not least to prevent undesirable practices but, as already mentioned, just as importantly to limit unnecessary delays. As a recent article in the *Spectator* (13 April 1991) pointed out: 'Each day wasted is a day lost to an unhappy child. The procedure should be as speedy as it is safe, and available as of right within a fixed time scale.'

Inter-country adoption must be firmly based on the principle that it is seen only as a temporary solution to a problem which is for the present insurmountable, and not as a means in the long term of solving the child-care problems of the donor country. Indeed, if inter-country adoption is to be a truly positive step, not only must the child in each case be gaining the best possible chance of security and happiness, but it is to be hoped that each arrangement will lead to improvements in social work practice in the host country. Where developing countries have been sending children to Europe, Canada, the USA and Australia for over thirty years, the country of origin does eventually use the infrastructure created and the experience gained to establish a culture of adoption in their own country. From this point of view it is essential that the birth countries should retain the initiative in the adoption process. The Hague Convention (on Private International Law) published a report on inter-country adoption in 1990 which noted that the emphasis had moved away from Asia to Latin America, as more Asian countries were introducing domestic adoption. Vietnam and Bangladesh have both prohibited adoption by foreigners, and India and Korea hope to be in a position to do so in the near future. Romania is not currently in this position and neither the Romanian authorities nor the orphanage relief agencies hold out much hope that many children will be reunited with their families.

When a specialist medical team organized by the Royal College of Psychiatrists returned from visiting Romania last autumn, Dr Ann Gath, the College's Registrar, reported:

> From what we saw and from what we heard in conversation with a variety of Romanians, it seems highly unlikely that homes will be found for these children in Romanian families because of the severe problems, economic and social, in the country. It would obviously be extremely sad to think of Romania providing children for a world market but under these exceptional circumstances the outlook for the children in their own country is extremely bleak. We would therefore recommend that the college did support adoption of these children and offered services to support the parents who undertake this task. The adoption of Romanian children by people from other countries should be for a limited period until Romania has sorted out its major social and economic problems.

Dr Ann Gath recognized that the provision of aid could not alone overcome the scale or nature of the problem. Her analysis was based on the judgment that no genuine alternatives actually exist. This is indeed the ultimate and sole criterion by which the admissibility of inter-country adoption should be judged and this is plainly stated by the United Nations (UN Convention on the Rights of the Child, November 1989):

The primary aim of adoption is to provide the child who cannot be cared for by his or her own parents with a permanent family. If that child cannot be placed in a foster or adoptive family and cannot in any suitable manner be cared for in the country of origin, inter-country adoption may be considered as an alternative means of child care.

Clearly, the crucial phrase is 'cannot in any suitable manner be cared for in the country of origin'. If this condition is to have been satis-factorily fulfilled, we do need to develop close channels of communi-cation with the sending countries. The law requires either that the natural parents formally consent to the adoption of their child, or that a certificate of abandonment is produced by the relevant authorities. This can prove to be difficult since there is contradictory information as well as conflicting opinion about the so-called 'availability' of some children. For example, I understand that there is some controversy at the moment about whether Romanian children should be adopted only from the orphanages or other institutions and not directly from their families. Some of the Social Services departments in this country maintain that there are in fact relatively few babies whose parents are prepared to relinquish them for adoption, and they have expressed concern about rumours that pregnant women are being approached. Other sources, including relief agencies, maintain that the number of children available for adoption is very high indeed. The Romanian Government believes that there are 170,000 children in orphanages and other establishments, but many of these are older children for whom adoption outside Romania is not an easy option.

Unless the sending country, in this case Romania, can establish a supervisory body which can monitor and organize the adoptions, access to reliable information will remain difficult. For this reason, the recent establishment of the Romanian Adoption Committee, which will act as a central authority, is hopefully a welcome move. The Romanian Government intends to provide a reassuring point of contact for the authorities in the receiving countries but is also well aware that the task of collecting information from the more remote institutions will take time. The Adoption Committee have so far registered 450 children as suitable for adoption by foreigners, which would appear to be only a tiny proportion of the overall figure. I was very pleased to be able to discuss this with the President of Romania when he was in London recently. President Iliescu made it quite clear that adoption by foreigners should continue to be considered for those children for whom it would appear to be the most sensible and humane choice. But he was not satisfied with the current procedures and said that they had certainly been abused. He wanted to see certain changes in the Romanian law to counteract the biggest enemy of all: baby trafficking.

The efforts being made in Romania highlight the need for an improved infrastructure in countries such as those of Central and South America. International legislation can play an important part in strengthening the ties of communication and preventing haphazard practice. The Special Commission of the Hague Conference on Private International Law is currently drafting a convention on inter-country adoption which, when signed by the fifty-two countries involved, will have significant effects on international co-operation. The convention recognizes the need for each participating country to establish a central authority which can be recognized by the other member states, while allowing for members to make their own internal arrangements (always provided that the overall legal standards are satisfied).

Some are cynical about the efficacy of such legislation. Agreement among delegates, they say, is one thing; enforcing the standards agreed or detecting when they have been violated is quite another. The Social Services departments in this country feel panicked because inter-country adoption, by definition, is not wholly within their control. They are asked to make lifelong decisions which will affect children whose background is unfamiliar to them. Indeed, the whole concept of international adoption presents a profound paradox for all the statutory organizations involved. As one social worker put it, 'Time spent on arranging an overseas adoption is time taken away from our statutory and primary duties of finding families for the children in our care.' Furthermore, carrying out this work throws into confusion current social work thinking, which does not encourage trans-racial placements. It is hard to reconcile arranging inter-country adoptions with decisions to keep black children in British institutions until black parents can be found for them, while turning away white parents. Perhaps the humanitarian message brought by increasing exposure to inter-country adoption will break down some of this strong feeling against trans-racial adoption.

Since I initially helped some couples to speed up their adoption of Romanian children, many others have written to me describing the problems they are facing. A worryingly high proportion have complained of the hostile manner in which they have been treated by their local authority. But it seems as if this is not just a problem identified with inter-country adoption but something more deep-rooted. As one mother wrote:

Resentment against the social services is not confined to overseas adopters. Many people I have spoken to who are adopting locally say they are treated not as partners in the community, not as responsible adults putting themselves forward for a responsible and difficult job, but as backward children themselves, as 'clients'.

And again:

They seem to believe that there are hordes of childless and desperate couples impulsively galloping off to Romania, Chile, Peru etc at the drop of a TV programme.

While adoption is primarily for the benefit of the child and secondly for the adult, the happiness of the one makes for the happiness of the other, and their needs must be seen as complementary. Many of the Social Services departments hold that families do not wish or intend to comply with the procedures and that they are often impatient and stubborn. And yet, all the people with whom I have been in contact express their desire to follow the system, but do not understand the procedures they are expected to follow and are not told how long it will take. Surely a change in attitude towards parenting and towards those who wish to parent is needed? Surely would-be adoptive parents should be reassured and informed so that they are not tempted to take the law into their own hands?

Perhaps some social workers feel defensive because they have been overwhelmed by requests not only to carry out home studies but to provide advice and information, often of a kind which they simply cannot give or do not have. I have called repeatedly for the setting-up of an independent but officially recognized helpline or information centre which can save time for social workers and act as a first port of call to those interested in the idea but who know virtually nothing. Such a service would have to provide reliable and up-to-date information about the countries offering children for adoption, and any changes in the procedures or legal requirements. Considerable expense would have to be anticipated if the service was to be useful, but it could hardly fail to save hours of precious social work time. This information service would not have the power to arrange adoptions and it should not be able to override the decision of a particular social worker, but it could help to minimize the inefficiency of the current system which is too heavily overburdened. Virginia Bottomley recognized the advantages of such a service, if it were to 'provide a safe, reliable and sympathetic source of preliminary advice for parents wanting to embark on that course' and so 'ensure that our response to these tragic circumstances safeguards the welfare of the children and enables public-spirited parents, who are properly equipped, to offer a long-term home to children who would otherwise have a distinctly bleak future'.

There seems to be a growing sense that Social Services personnel must listen harder to those for whom they provide services. At a recent conference on inter-country adoption (which I organized with Baroness Faithfull, Chairman of the All Party Parliamentary Group for Children), Sheila Conway, the Director of Childlink, stressed the importance of 'building bridges' between prospective adopters and the adoption agencies. I agree that the opinions of those who have experienced the system at first hand must be listened to if the system is going to be improved. For this reason, I was very happy to become one of the Vice-Presidents of the Campaign for Intercountry Adoption (CICA) which is an all-party lobby group made up principally of parents who have adopted from abroad. The group has already proved its worth; several meetings have been set up with Government ministers, and a very useful and constructive meeting took place between CICA and President Iliescu and his advisers.

There is indeed a great deal of family-to-family support in this country and I have met many enterprising and dedicated parents who are determined that their children will understand and appreciate their own background and cultural history. STORK, the association for families who have adopted from abroad, has a membership of over two hundred families with children represented from at least twenty countries. Other groups such as the El Salvador Family Association and the newly established Association for Romanian Children plan a range of events, from children's parties to educational videos about the country from where the child has been adopted.

Families have played their part in ensuring that these children have the best chance possible of a healthy start. Associations, committees, campaign groups, consultation documents are all important, and so are the procedures and regulations that protect these children. But as was recently pointed out by a writer in the *Guardian* (13 November 1990), 'It is high time coherent and consensual policy is put in place if children's best interests, to which everyone pays lip service, are to be truly served.' It is no longer adequate or realistic for child welfare organizations and adoption agencies to uphold the dogma that transracial placements are inherently undesirable. In an ideal world, children should not only remain in the country of their origin but with their natural parents. In reality, while the alternative is years of institutionalized misery at best and total abandonment and death at worst, the question of ethnicity and culture remains noble rhetoric. Of course, as adopted children grow into adulthood, they will want to understand their background and original circumstances. Yet if we are truly and firmly committed to the idea that children belong with a family of their own, it is tender loving care that alone can overcome the traumas of a child who has been genuinely abandoned.

Index